A COSMIC DIALOGUE

Reassessing Methods for Understanding New Planets

Patricia Garner

Published in 2016 by Raven Dreams Productions
1434 NE Prescott St
Portland, OR 97211
www.ravendreamspress.com

ISBN 978-0-9840474-8-2

Cover photo by NASA

Printed in the United States of America

TABLE OF CONTENTS

TABLE OF CONTENTS

ACKNOWLEDGEMENT

This publication would never have made it past square one without the inspired, well-informed and compassionate assistance of Adam Gainsburg. Gary Caton was also generous in sharing his astrological and astronomical insights. The work of Bernadette Brady, MA, has been critical in lifting my eyes from the ecliptic and into the vast, beautiful universe of celestial bodies.

Anyone who reads this publication will realize that I owe a great debt of gratitude to the writings of Nicholas Campion. I deeply admire and give credit to the open-mindedness and astronomical acumen of the most prolific celestial body discoverer, Dr. Michael E. Brown. Thank you Philip Sedgwick for letting me know about his discoveries; you set me on a great path. Tony Howard did me the great honor of being willing to get my message out into the world. Last but by no means the least, I acknowledge the support of my husband and beloved partner Bennett. He provided me exactly what was needed at the moment – listening to more astrological and astronomical esoterica, encouraging me when my solo research seemed like shouting into the wind, and loving me when I needed it the most. As one can see, I have been able to avail myself of many sources – As Around, So Within.

FOREWORD

It is time for the astrological community to step back and more fully appreciate that for decades we have allowed astronomers to designate the astrological significance of celestial bodies. This was most likely not the intent of astronomers, or astrologers, but this is what happened and continues to happen. The process goes as follows: individual astronomers select a name and we astrologers adopt the name. Without further ado, we take the archetypal and mythological meaning that is historically ascribed *to that name* and *presto*—we have a new astrological significator. This process may constitute a feat of notable legerdemain, but by endorsing astronomers' names for these new bodies as if they were an astrological *fait accompli*, we ignore our tradition's proven excellence in conferring astrological significance. We skip right past the most basic steps—carefully observing the new body and forming conclusions based on these observations and our professional experience. These were the steps our ancestors took in identifying and ascribing significance to planetary bodies, which achievements ultimately furnished the foundations that have defined astrology for millennia. We have utterly failed to come near, much less heed this well proven course. Importantly, as if our current omissions are not sufficiently problematic, they underscore another problem—our failure to interpret what the sudden appearance of a massive amount of new celestial bodies means to modern astrological practice. The explosion of celestial objects is just that, an explosion, but we are not thinking or talking about the implications of these events in a coordinated, co-informed manner within our field. This book represents an effort to stimulate the astrological community to undertake this exploration. I believe we must confront these issues, or be subsumed by them. We may no longer need to propitiate the deities, but we need not go so far as to relegate celestial beings to husks of their former selves.

INTRODUCTION

Flaws in How New Celestial Bodies Were Named: The Need for Astrological Assessment

Many of us may react to these statements by saying that if the names for the newly discovered bodies are okay for astronomers, then they should be okay for us. To me, this approach reflects a distressing level of complacence and denigrates the powerful truths that define our craft. It also prevents us from examining celestial designations from an *astrological* perspective. This is exciting stuff here! Our universe has transformed from being populated by few relatively similar entities to one brimming with a boundless number of diverse celestial objects. A pinprick of data viewed through the Hubble telescope reveals thousands of galaxies where each contains a "celestial continent of billions of stars." [1] Admittedly, our astrological reach may not extend quite that far, but at the very least and as square one, we have the opportunity to examine whether our reliance on the names astronomers have already chosen for new celestial bodies rests on firm foundations. As we will see, it does not. Scrutiny of these naming processes erodes, rather than bolsters, confidence we might have in the legitimacy of the significations. Largely because the astronomer who "discovers" a planetary body also names it, the naming stakes are high. The converse is also true: once the astronomical community accepts a name, it means the namer has been acknowledged to have "discovered" the planetary body—a rather chicken and egg methodology, but also one which underscores the competition among astronomers to attain "discoverer" status. As we might anticipate, these naming processes are characterized by the interplay of individual agendas and parochial interests. They also stand in stark contrast to the classical planets, where a millennia's worth of astronomical observation and inter-cultural exchanges coalesced into astrological identities. As noted by the late astrologer and historian James Herschel Holden,

> "Ideally, the influence of a celestial object would be determined from its observed effects in many charts. But the method most in vogue is to suppose that the name of the object is the key to its influence. This may sometimes be the case. But are we prepared to assume that among the asteroids Oceana influences sailors, Hygiea sanitation workers, Limburgia cheese-merchants, and Fanatica protesters and terrorists? And what shall we suppose to be the significance of Beagle, Brambilla,

Esperanto, Fanny, Jean-Jacques, Li, Rust-hawelia, Tynka, and Wrubel?" [2]

Astrologers Asking Questions Generates A New Astrological Litmus Test

We may also be tempted to ask: what's the big deal here? It is not as if we can wait for a millennia's worth of observations before names can be bestowed upon celestial entities, and not every home is equipped with state-of-the art astrophotograpic equipment. They are appearing now. Or, our charts may be getting a little crowded, but we can stem the celestial profusion by arriving at some reasonable trigger point or context for determining whether a body warrants astrological significance. I heartily endorse the latter endeavor, which in major part, constitutes why I am raising these issues. As we will see, however, the questions do not stop there. Naming flaws do not begin and end with asteroids. The processes by which Uranus and Neptune obtained their names do not paint a pretty picture either, and while more appealing, Pluto's naming is about as antithetical to Pluto's personality as it can get. Astronomers were undoubtedly aware of the mythological underpinnings for the classical planets when they named the modern ones, but as we have seen, their interests were heavily laden with efforts to obtain planetary discovery "bragging rights." What better way to go about it, and thereby secure their position for posterity than by completing the Greco-Roman pantheon? Uranus is the father of Saturn, and Neptune and Pluto are Jupiter's brothers. Thus anointed, they easily slide into our charts and our field's assumption that astrology provides the language for a dialogue between the earth and cosmos. We astrologers can also legitimately claim that Uranus, Neptune and Pluto seem to be doing quite well on the astrological front. Am I now saying that Uranus and Neptune should join Pluto in being somehow reclassified? Or worse—should naming flaws require us to purge their current astrological identities? Or, are these planets correctly named but for the wrong reasons—"wrong" being defined by previous perspectives and yard sticks? As to the first and second questions, I offer an unequivocal no; but being rightly named while not adhering to the classical pattern, an equally unequivocal yes.

All is not lost. I propose that astrological legitimacy does not solely or primarily attach to Uranus, Neptune and Pluto because of physical features, but lies instead in the concurrence between the timing of their respective discoveries and the themes embodied in contemporaneously occurring worldwide events. These events were momentous and spawned profound social and cultural changes whose impacts are still being experienced centuries later. The connections between the events and the planetary discoveries are, of course, widely acknowledged by mundane astrologers, but their importance here does not reside in keyword associations or traditional planetary correspondences, but with an entirely different lens and litmus. *The difference is that the relevant synchronicities or correspondences, and hence the essential substrate that legitimizes our acceptance of these planetary bodies in astrology, arises from a historically different foundation or source of authenticity.* In this context, mundane analyses may confirm or rule out modern planetary identities, but they do not in and of themselves establish significance. This is a difference of cosmology, of a broader epistemology, where the medium of the process contains the message. Exploration of this perspective reveals that the underlying theme embedded in these planetary "discoveries" is that as astrologers and human beings, we need to expand our focus and pay greater attention to the state of being of our world, the Earth, and the whole of humanity that occupies it. Isn't that what our understanding of the "outer" planets is all about anyway? Rather than solely espousing an ego-, ethno- or nation-centric paradigm, the universe is urging us to extend our horizons and to appreciate a world- or terra-centric dimension of experience, sensitivity and insight. Enter astrology, or, Enter a more inclusive, informed astrology! This is not to say that we should abandon healthy ego development or discard the value of cultural and social differences, but we also need to broaden our mindsets and attitudes. Much as in a hologram—ego and global levels co-exist with and mutually inform one another. They remind us that there are greater forces that provide meaning and texture.

Implications of the Sudden
Appearance of New Celestial Bodies:
The Post-Pluto Paradigm Shift

As if my proposal to legitimize modern planets' astrological significance on the basis of world events is not sufficiently heretical, I believe that the sudden appearance of a massive amount of new celestial bodies in and of itself raises profound questions for astrological exploration. It is not simply whether each body or group of bodies has justifiably attained astrological significance, which is important enough, but *why are they entering into our field of view now? And, what is the meaning of their emergence?* Importantly, an intrinsic feature of this solar system reorientation is the "demotion" of Pluto. And yet, *while most of us acknowledge the reclassification of Pluto, we have not paid commensurate attention to the meaning of the reclassification itself.* I contend that Pluto's downgrade, or "Post-Pluto," constitutes a cosmic exclamation point to the sentence written by the discoveries of Uranus, Neptune and Pluto. As such, it heralds a paradigm shift tantamount to Copernicus' depiction of a heliocentric rather than a geocentric solar system. In sum, Post-Pluto up-dates and amplifies the *"As Above, So Below"* archetype that has informed much of modern astrology by suggesting a new dimension—*"As Around, So Within."*

At its most basic level, Pluto's demotion means that a planet we thought was a planet is no longer a planet. As if this event is not sufficient to convince us that we are no longer in Kansas, it is also the case that the solar system we thought was a solar system is no longer the solar system. In the millennia before Pluto lost its full planetary status in 2006, most people, including astronomers and astrologers, believed that our solar system was populated with a few, bigger-than-big planets. Human beings were here and non-Earth celestial entities were out there, and in order to bridge the two, we had to [eventually] rocket into space. However, as recognized by the astronomical community, Pluto's reclassification represents a "revolution in the geography of the solar system." [3] According to this model, we no longer occupy a solar system based on discrete planetary entities, but one populated by belts and zones of celestial bodies of all shapes and sizes. As discussed above, while our awareness of Uranus, Neptune and Pluto's discoveries connotes, "*we're all in this _world_ together*," Post-Pluto significantly ups the ante by signaling that "*we're all in this _solar system_ together*."

This said, there is more to the maxim of "*As Around, So Within*," and much of it stems from the timing of these celestial events. The first act of the "*As Around, So Within*" drama consists of centuries-long development of planetary identities. Act II was launched when Uranus, Neptune and Pluto came on the scene and took roughly 149 years to complete. At that time we were directed towards worldwide events that had momentous impact on human beings and the Earth on which they resided. The official announcement of Pluto's demotion, that simultaneously reconfigured the structure of our solar system, took place in one day. These celestial events exhibit a tempo and thereby tell a story. As such, they presuppose the existence of an underlying design or pattern—the play itself. Most astrologers are familiar with the concept of *"As Above, So Below,"* and at the very least, these events re-confirm the veracity of this adage. In particular, it reminds us of an often forgotten part of the statement that suggests a whole, a unity or an underlying principle that connects the *"Above"* and the *"Below."* I also contend that the progressive broadening of our awareness that these celestial events connote also reflects the cosmos trying to get its point across: *As Around, So Within.* Or, our awareness of the new celestial configuration parallels the cosmos' awareness of its new configuration. As recognized by the astrologer and historian Dr. Robert Hand, astrology recognizes the "universe as a living entity . . . where psyche and cosmos are one." [4] Post-Pluto tells us that as the cosmos is around and within us, so we are around and within the cosmos. Not up there and down here, but we each animate and stimulate the consciousness of the other by participating in a process of co-creation.

The Importance of Astrologically Defined Astrology

Convincing astronomers of the viability of astrology is also not the point, as that implicitly suggests that we cannot come to the table of interstellar discovery in our own right and with our own perspectives. Our telescopes may not be mounted in Flagstaff or Mauna Kea, but our observations are no less valid. If we "rock the boat," so be it. On the other hand, conspiratorially winking at each other as if we are the sole keepers of true sky wisdom does not describe a very wise course either. Astronomy is our long-lost sibling, a reunion with which would advance both fields considerably. *The point here is that we need to develop and apply an <u>astrological</u> litmus to astronomical discoveries.* We must articulate our own truths and our own standards. If we fail to do so, the chance of establishing the profound relevance of our unique contributions will continue to be seriously diminished. If everything has significance, then nothing has significance. As articulated by astrologer, historian and teacher Bernadette Brady, M.A., at the 2005 Annual Conference of the Astrological Association of Great Britain, the surge in adding new planetary bodies to our charts represents something of a "pluralistic philosophy without knowing what we are really doing," and may undermine rather than confirm the significance of planetary energies and their consonances. [5] Why would astronomers or the public listen to us if we fail to respect ourselves? I believe we must confront these issues, or be subsumed by them. We need to boldly go where we want to go, and as I hope to show in this book, engaging in that enterprise leads to some very interesting places. [6]

1

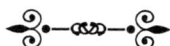

The Proliferation of Celestial Bodies: A Gauntlet Flung at Astrology

Celestial Excess

Our charts now routinely feature everything from Ceres to Sedna, the Great Attractor and at least five of the Centaurs. Our challenge, unprecedented in 6,000 years of practice, is to navigate a population of celestial objects that number in the hundreds of thousands (and more). Indeed, it is important to appreciate the fact that today we distinguish "celestial objects" from "planetary bodies"—not to mention the differences between asteroids in general and Trans-Neptunians, Kuiper Belt Objects or even Centaurs.

A popular t-shirt in astrological circles today reads, "I still remember in my day there were only 9 planets." Fortunately or not, we cannot turn that clock back. This development signals not simply the addition of newly discovered celestial objects into our understanding of the solar system, but populating our celestial maps with new *categories* of entities. The process is rather like pulling rabbits from a magician's hat. How do we pull elephants or dark matter from the same hat? And what is the hat and who is the magician? Not only do we struggle to keep up with what is really out there, but more importantly, what are the rules for identifying and qualifying new bodies into consistent categories?

Even to astronomers, the classification of celestial objects results in overlapping and often confusing labels for the same bodies. Plutinos—not to be confused with plutoids or plutons—are a family of Trans Neptunian Objects (TNO's) that have the same 2:3 orbital resonance with Neptune as Pluto's. [7] (There are also Twotinos, which have a 2:1 orbital resonance with Neptune.) This category has nothing to do with other features, only their orbits. TNO's are Kuiper Belt Objects (KBO's) due to their location within the Kuiper Belt, or about 30-50 astronomical units from the Sun. There are also other TNO-KBO's called cubewanos or Classical Kuiper Belt Objects, but their orbits are outside Neptune's and not resonant with it. Plutoids are TNO dwarf planets, or bodies orbiting beyond Neptune, but are identified by their shape—

round. Some astronomers prefer to call them "ice dwarfs," and although the International Astronomical Union ("IAU") recognizes that there are likely thousands of plutoids. It has only named four: Pluto, Eris, Haumea, and Makemake. [8] Of course, satellites of plutoids are not plutoids themselves, "even if they are massive enough that their shape is dictated by self-gravity," i.e. they are round. The IAU defines a Scattered Disk Object (SDO) as being "scattered" by Neptune's gravitational strength. Sedna is classified by the IAU as a SDO, but does not come near enough to Neptune to have been "scattered" by it. Eris is the most massive dwarf planet in the solar system, but it is a trans-Neptunian planet or Scattered Disk object, depending on whether one is gauging relative importance by orbit or size. One might ask at this point—has our attention span become sufficiently glazed over?

Our problems do not stop here, and instead take us all the way back to fundamental astrological assumptions. What constitutes a planet in the first place? With whom were we really playing all these years? Recent astronomical discoveries have revealed that a planet we surely thought was a planet turns out not to be one. These revelations may have transpired because the astronomical community was attempting to calm the feather ruffling that surrounded the demotion of Pluto, but uncertainty persists. Although one probably does not want to "mess around" with Pluto, it is also true that, as recognized in legal parlance—"bad facts make bad law." This truism says that a tragedy makes us sympathetic and triggers our desire to make it right for the victims, but leaning over backward in one situation may create terrible consequences in other situations and for society as a whole. Or, "a badly defined Sedna makes a badly defined SDO."

We can obtain no solace from the planetary proliferation dilemma by relying on the fact that astronomers have at least resolved what constitutes a planet. In 2006 the International Astronomical Union ("IAU") declared that a planet is an object which orbits the Sun, has sufficient mass for its self gravity to allow it to assume a nearly round shape, and has "cleared the neighborhood" around its orbit. [9] Unfortunately, this standard was adopted at the end of the conference when only 400 of the 10,000 IAU members were still attending and voted. Vigorous disagreements among astronomers linger about what constitutes a planet. If this test were applied to Neptune, Jupiter, Mars, and Earth—none would pass the "full clearance" test. There are some 10,000 asteroids that orbit near Earth, and Jupiter can boast of 100,000 such bodies. Earth and Jupiter may be "dynamically dominant," due to their mass, but they do not "clear" their respective orbital paths. [10] For that matter, what about the Moon vis-à-vis the Earth? Pluto also crosses Neptune's orbit, so has Neptune failed to clear its orbit? [11] There are problems with the "relatively spherical shape" guideline as well. Haumea is oblong or cigar shaped, but if rotated more slowly, it would be spherical. Another problem is that the 2006 IAU definition did not preclude nuclear fusion from being a planetary body's power source, which means that stars can be planets too. [12] Noting that an icy celestial body becomes round due to its mass, or "somewhere between 200 and 400 km," the renowned California Institute of Technology astronomer and asteroid-discoverer Dr. Michael E. Brown declares that under current schema there should be "no iceball left behind." He adds,

> "It is hard to make a consistent argument that a 400-km iceball should count as a planet because it might have interesting geology, while a 5000-km satellite with a massive atmosphere, methane lakes, and dramatic storms (Titan) shouldn't be put into the same category, whatever you call it." [13]

In an interesting nuance that demonstrates how confounding astronomical taxonomy can be, dwarf planets may not exactly be what we think they are. The 2006 IAU General Assembly distinguished between "planets" and "dwarf planets." These quotation marks are _not_ supplied by me, but by the IAU. As we have seen, a "planet" defines a celestial body as one that orbits the sun, is round, and has cleared the neighborhood around its orbit. A "dwarf planet" is a celestial body that orbits the Sun, is nearly round, but has not cleared the neighborhood and is not a satellite. [14] The IAU lists a third and final category that broadly refers to "solar system bodies, which are all other objects orbiting the Sun, except satellites." At first blush and since the word "planet" is used for both entities, it would appear that the IAU thereby designated two categories of planets—major (such as Earth, Jupiter, Uranus, etc.) and dwarf (currently-Ceres, Pluto, Eris, Makemake and Haumea). That is not the case. The IAU explicitly separated "dwarf planet" into an entirely distinct category. A dwarf planet is therefore not a planet; it is a dwarf planet. Noted astronomer Dr. Alex Filippenko has suggested one solution to this problem, e.g. we may wish to borrow from Isaac Asimov's playbook and use the term "mesoplanet" for these entities. [15] Michael Brown highlights the "something that looks like a planet, but is not a planet" definition of dwarf planets and states that current technology has yet to determine the number of dwarf planets. In an attempt to solve this dilemma, he suggests that planetary objects should be categorized by those which can be determined to be planets with near certainty, or are highly likely, likely, probably and possibly planets. [16] For example, the "near certainty" category includes Eris, Pluto, Haumea, Makemake, etc.; as "highly likely," Brown lists Ixion and Salacia; Varuna is a "probable," and Chiriklo, Ceto and Chiron are "possibly" planetary objects.

The matter of celestial numerosity is not going to get any clearer any time soon. On the contrary, astronomical research indicates that we have literally discovered the iceberg's tip of celestial bodies. In January 2016, scientists announced they had detected a Neptune-sized planet—not just a planetary object or dwarf planet, but a planet—with an elliptical, 15,000-year orbit around the sun. [17] In May 2013, astronomers using data from NASA's Wide-field Infrared Survey Explorer "WISE" identified 28 new *families* of asteroids. [18] NASA scientists have hypothesized that there may be "dozens or even more than 100 dwarf planets awaiting discovery." It appears that our galaxy contains at least as many planets as stars. Nine hundred planets have been discovered, and "a few thousand others are under investigation." [19] More fertile stellar fields beckon, as most of the huge telescopes that have been successful in discovering newer celestial entities are primarily tuned into bodies viewable from the Northern Hemisphere. Remarkably, Michael Brown highlights the 12,000-year elliptical orbit of Sedna, which means that using present astronomical technology, there was only a 200-year window within which we could have discovered her. [20] Such impossibly long orbits mean an impossibly large number of cosmic companions that await our discernment. I like the analogy made by University of California, Berkeley astronomer Geoff Marcy who indicates that the "universe is jam-packed, like jelly beans in a jar." [21] And at one time or another we thought we might be alone!

In sum and as all of us have likely noticed, even if we may not have wanted to—there are dwarf and proto planets, plutoids, Trans Neptunian objects, asteroids, centaurs, Trojans, Scattered Disk Objects, black holes, quasars and most assuredly, more to come. Every day various classifications seem to grow—we now have Greeks and Hildas as well as Trojans occupying the inner solar system. The largest of the centaurs between Mars and Jupiter is not Chiron but Chariklo. Although we increasingly hear of Ceres, Pallas Athene, Vesta and Juno, it appears that the first 3 of these minor planets plus Hygiea, and not Juno, account for about half of the solar system asteroid mass. Planets outside our solar system, or exoplanets, have also been identified. What will we do with wormhole sites and other time-space anomalies? What about the fact that 99.9% of the solar system is empty, and 99% of that amount is taken up with the Sun. [22] Should space itself be considered as an entity? Clearly, this is a massive, paradigm-shifting glut of new information.

We Need to Take a Breather

The first step in grappling with the recent explosion of astronomical data and the astrological models which attempt to interpret them is that we need to call a moratorium on populating astrological charts with every latest celestial body. We should refrain from serially adding each new bit of information without good reason, or simply adopting astronomical nomenclature without commensurate astrological assessment. Fear of "missing the boat" or getting left behind our colleagues is not a sufficient reason. As we tamp down our tendency to embrace all incoming tides of information, the hubbub subsides. A space then opens that frees us to embark upon a process of self and professional reflection about astrology's current standing and future direction. Once we initiate this assessment, however, nothing should be off the table and no subject or astrological perspective should be so sacred as to avoid an earnest examination. The fact that astrology is largely understood by the public or the scientific community as outside the mainstream should not dissuade us from determining valid astrological meaning from those newly-discovered bodies with which we are interested. We should also not be fearful of disagreeing with each other. This is admittedly a huge undertaking, with an uncertain ending. Astrology needs a retrograde space of its own, and we will hopefully reap the fruits of these labors with a reinvigorated vision of our place in the universe.

I have done my best to find astrologers who have taken an in-depth look at the challenge posed to astrology by the proliferation of celestial bodies, and have found one. It is presented in an article *Asteroids and Mythic Astrology* written by archetypal and Hellenistic astrologer Demetra George. [23] It is a commendable and courageous attempt to tackle our predicament, and I hope to address it in that same spirit. Her answer is that, contrary to the post-Ptolemaic reliance on physical and scientific explanations, the mythic tradition is "a valid philosophical approach by which to delineate the interpretive significance of celestial bodies in chart analysis." [24] The first shortcoming with this approach is that it limits resolution by suggesting an unsatisfying either—or choice [science or astrology]. More importantly, it fails to determine which myth or symbol should be applied to which asteroid or celestial object, and why. Myths arising from the collective unconscious indubitably confer identity and meaning, even more profoundly than "objective" categorizations, but this assertion sidesteps the dilemma. Such a process names first and assigns symbolic meaning second. Just because a name is rooted in mythology does not instantly confer significance, nor does it mean we should allow the tail to wag the dog. We need to look before we name.

2

The Importance of Naming

Step One—A Bit of Philosophy

At this point, it is important to spend a moment or two pondering the influence of naming and nomenclature, or the implications of calling one celestial body Jupiter or Venus and another Chiron or Lilith. This endeavor may be epistemological, but failing to engage in it may eventually undermine the ultimate attribution of astrological significance to celestial bodies. It also does not require the exquisite sensitivities of an astrologer to recognize that naming and symbol-making intrinsically wield considerable power. Names are big deals. They not only provide context and category, but establish substance and character as well. Not to mention astrological significance.

Names categorize, identify and confer meaning. They allow us to distinguish one thing or idea from another. Naming becomes more complicated when we move from an object that is directly observable, such as an "apple" or "star" to an entity that is more conceptual, potentially ambiguous.

Recent research has demonstrated that emotions play an important role in how human beings learn and remember. At the very least, words contain emotional overlays about which we may be largely unaware. [25] They are complicated creatures that are designed to invoke and arouse human reaction.

Words are undeniably construed on the basis of a variety of factors, including social and cultural perspectives, but this circumstance does not eliminate their intrinsic meaning-making quality. In fact, our awareness of this feature of words should be in the forefront of our assessment of celestial body nomenclature.

Conferring a name on an object or idea not only identifies or defines it, but can impart reality as well. By doing so, it provides an internal mental structure or architecture within which we navigate our observations and experiences. Because names create reality, we also assume the names we assign things are true, or characterizing what the thing actually is. We do not have to "think twice" about names because we apprehend and perceive them as the state of being that we have named.

A corollary to the "reality principle" of naming is that we can become so attached to our labels that we miss critical information that we might otherwise perceive. This is the siege mentality that can surface when one believes that their way is not only the right way, but the *only* way. This is the "I am right, you are wrong" quality that can surface when, for example, a paradigm based upon astrology meets with astronomy, and vice versa.

As all of us have likely experienced, once perceptions are set, they are resistant to change. A fascinating feature about this perseverance is that if we are verbally told how to do something, as opposed to working it out for ourselves through trial-and-error, we are much less likely to modify our outlook. [26] When we learn from "recognized experts," humans become even more impervious to behavioral revision. If astrologers are told that Pluto is a planet but new information challenges that view, the fact that we have been told Pluto is a planet makes us more resistant to reevaluation.

As science fiction author Philip K. Dick warns, "[t]he basic tool for the manipulation of reality is the manipulation of words. If you can control the meaning of words, you can control the people who must use the words." [27]

The Importance of Naming in Astrology

Naming occupies a particularly fundamental place in astrology. In many ways, it represents the sum and substance, the very essence of astrology. We use significators to assess significance, and planets constitute touchstones for significance. Astrological naming is, of course, not immune from the vagaries of any naming process. Not only do planetary names identify celestial objects, but we apprehend the reality and personality of them through these lenses. Once adopted, these labels frame our astrological knowledge and experience. We may feel a sense of comfort with Ceres-Demeter's evocation of maternal, unconditional love, but the same spirit does not accompany the names "Eris" or "Kali," much less "Trish."[28] Or, as eloquently stated by astrologer and writer Liz Greene,

> "Perhaps the most important key of all is that we love astrology not merely for its own sake, or for the comfort it brings, but for what its language points to, what its doors open onto, and what its symbols awaken in us as a recollection of where we have come from and where we are going."[29]

To be clear, the problem here is not that the names we have chosen for newly discovered celestial bodies have no "objective" basis, or alternatively, that they tap into intangible, archetypal or collective understandings. To our credit, we freely acknowledge our employment of a complex brew of archetypal imaging and meaning-making when infusing celestial objects with Earth-bound qualities. It is because, not in spite, of the fact that we draw from such formidable wellsprings that we must exercise caution when articulating consonances between the human or collective psyche, and celestial bodies.

3

❦·—∞—·❦

The Ancient Paradigm Supporting Classical Planets' Astrological Legitimacy

Before examining the deficiencies in how recently discovered celestial bodies have been and continue to be named, it is important to appreciate the context within which the classical planets were named. When we understand how planetary naming *has* historically taken place, we may better equip ourselves to apprehend and articulate astrological guideposts that can be used in naming proliferating celestial bodies, as well as to assist us in identifying what might be missing or is extraneous to our current *modus operandi*. In undertaking this examination, we will be looking at the question: what has the "-ology" which follows "astro-" meant throughout the millennia, and, by extension, what does this history say about the astrological foundation within which celestial bodies might be legitimately nested today? This question subsumes another: what has traditionally been the relationship between astronomy and astrology, and how might that nexus—or lack thereof—affect our current dilemma?

Principal Features in identifying and Naming Classical Planets

Direct Observation

The first step the ancients likely took in developing astrological acuity was to look UP and experience the profound marvels of the sky. These were keen observations, not obscured by smog or the indoor focus of contemporary life. It may be difficult to appreciate today, but one can only imagine how starkly intimate this undertaking must have been. Without clocks or calendars, weeks or weekends, much less an established zodiac, house system or astronomical library telling them that the moving lights were other bodies just like Earth sharing the Sun as their orbital center, the ancients enjoyed a kind of transparency with the cosmos very difficult for most of us to imagine today. In looking above, our ancestors breathed under a myriad of moving points of light. Some light points remained in the same relationship to each other, forming fixed, familiar patterns or constellations ["con" = "together" or "with"]. Others traced irregular patterns across the wide bowl of the sky. These are our modern day "planets," which word stems from the Greek verb *planetein*, meaning "to wander." [30] Perhaps even more evocative are *planetein*'s Babylonian linguistic roots—"sheep who escape from the fold." [31] Even today, many of us count sheep in order to slip into slumber!

Sky events also regularly correlated with daily and seasonal occurrences, which in turn signaled when to plant and harvest life-sustaining nourishment. The regular rising of planets and stars heralded their birth, while setting below the horizons signaled their demise. Centuries of observations demonstrated that the planets appeared in different parts of the sky and at differing times of the year. Qualities such as relative brightness or color, length of visibility and proximity to fixed stars distinguished the different entities, which observations served as first steps towards establishing planetary names and underlying meaning.

Given the indispensable relationship our forebears experienced between the cosmos and terrestrial affairs, humans understandably sought indications of celestial order. Exactly when these associations coalesced is, of course, lost in antiquity, as is the date when modern humans began avoiding them. The indications of "emergent order" were clearly reflected in the ancients' efforts to organize planets and stars into familiar groupings or stories. [32] The "wanderers" played their respective parts on the constellational stages, as recognized by the star stories that human legends are made of—and the human legends that star stories are made of.

Sky Studies Took Place Early and Often

In his *Chronology of the Astrology of the Middle East and West by Period*, Robert Hand notes the impossibility of setting a precise date for the earliest planetary observations, but also cites a point in time before 15,000 BCE (Paleolithic period) when humans first chronicled "phases of the Moon by making scratches on pieces of bone." [33] Archeologists have recently discovered a circle or "calendar" of 12 pits created during the Mesolithic period (10,000—5,000 BCE) that mimics the phases of the Moon. [34] While not uniformly acknowledged, there is also evidence of recording moon cycles dating back to 30,000 BCE. [35]

Impressive examples of the attention the ancients devoted to the cyclic nature of sky events are found a number of Babylonian astronomical texts, including the astrolabes or "star lists arranged in a circular or rectangular order," the *MUL.APIN* [*mul-* "star," *mul*-an—"heavenly star," c. 1000 BCE) catalogue, and the *Enuma Anu Enlil (*c. 600 BCE) omen series. [36] In analyzing these compendia of celestial happenings, early Babylonian astronomers did not see their sky as an abstract celestial sphere that was described by geometric computation and longitudinal lines, nor did they have access to the concept of an equator. [37] Rather, they were interested in discerning their cosmos through the celestial happenings that lay before their eyes. Over time, they not only observed celestial bodies and events, as well as a coordinate system based on "cubit" or "finger" distance from certain stars (the "Normal Stars"), but the underlying patterns and relationships that arose between them. These were the "synodic moments" or moments of re-connection, which included recurring phenomena of heliacal risings and settings which were so central to the Babylonian framework. [38] It may seem rather obvious to us that the sky expresses itself through regular, periodic movements, but this was a profound discovery that continues to inform today's astrology and astronomy. [39] The MUL.APIN enumerated eighteen zodiacal constellations that we would likely recognize today. [40] It does not take much imagination to appreciate the generations of sky watchers that it took to arrive at the following data,

"Subjects found in the *MUL.APIN* include names and relative positions in the sky of fixed stars, dates of their heliacal risings, simultaneous risings and settings of certain stars and constellations, so-called *ziqpu* stars that cross the zenith of the observer, stars in the path of the moon, astronomical seasons, luni-solar intercalation rules with fixed stars, stellar calendar, appearances and disappearances of the five planets (Mercury, Venus, Mars, Jupiter and Saturn), periods of visibility and invisibility of the planets, length of daylight scheme, and lunar visibility scheme." [41]

The focus upon celestial, and particularly lunar, relationships continued in the *Enuma Anu Enlil* and by 600 BCE Babylonian astronomers had, for example, collected sufficient information to predict the Saros cycle (223 synodic months or 18 years) of lunar eclipses. [42]

The *MUL.APIN* calculations continued to serve as the "backbone of astronomical knowledge up until the time of Kepler." [43] Although there is no extant copy of his treatise, Plato's student Eudoxus of Cnidus (406-355 BCE) used the Babylonian sidereal framework to describe the constellations, which was then cited by the Stoic philosopher Aratus of Soloi (c 300 BCE) in compiling a similar work, the *Phenomena*. [44] This information made its way to Hipparchus (c. 190-126 BCE), as evidenced by his work *Commentary on Aratus*. Ptolemy (c. 70 CE) makes specific reference to Hipparchus in his star catalogue, the *Almagest*. To close the circle, in 1992, when it officially designated the number and names for our constellations, the International Astronomical Union explicitly relied on Ptolemy's *Almagest*. [45]

The early importance of ongoing celestial cycles is also demonstrated by the arrangement of prominent stones or megaliths ["mega"=large, "lith"=stone] that trace lines of sight to mark summer and winter solstices. These include, for example, Stonehenge, Avebury and some 900 other stone circles in the British Isles dating at least as far back as 3,600 BCE. If single standing stones are considered, the number is much higher. [46] The Egyptian site at Nabta Playa contains a stone "calendar circle" (4,950 BCE) that marks solstices, and in particular, correlates the summer solstice with the onset of the rains that filled the Nile and denoted time for planting. Stones that lie under the temples at Hagar Qum and Mnajdra, Malta, dating from 3,600 to 2,500 BCE, have also been shown to align with Pleiades' heliacal risings. [47]

Astrology and Astronomy Were Partners In Defining Celestial Order

Repeated correlations between sky-based and human cycles confirmed, or in more modern parlance— "proved," the ancient's apprehension of a cosmic unity, as well as the character of the planetary entities that operated within it. These empirical observations also allowed humans to calculate what actions they needed to take in order act in accordance with the underlying cosmic plan. This is astrology, where humans anticipated events in order to more effectively navigate their environment. As articulated by astrologer and historian Nicholas Campion, "astrology is invariably a guide to action." [48] Babylonian historian N. M. Swerdlow also writes,

"It was believed in antiquity that astronomy, including celestial divination, was the most ancient science, and this with good reason. According to Josephus (*Ant. Jud.* 1.69-72), the knowledge of the heavens was discovered by the descendants of Seth, who inscribed all they found on two pillars, one of brick, the other of stone, so that if the former were destroyed in the Deluge, as in fact came to pass, the latter would survive to teach men what was written on it. And so God so loved these Patriarchs of wisdom that for the sake of the usefulness of their knowledge of astronomy and geometry he granted them very long lives, for had they not lived for 600 years, the period of a "Great Year," they could have foretold nothing with certainty (1.106)." [49]

An early example of the complex, interconnected nature of the predictive process can be found in the Babylonian 70-tablet *Enuma Anu Enlil*, including the 63rd tablet, the famous Venus Tablet of *Ammisaduqa*, dating from the seventh century BCE. [50] The forecasts articulated in these tablets were framed in the form of "omens," generally consisting of a protasis or if-clause linked to a visual event in the sky, and an apodosis, or a then-clause relating to a human event on Earth. [51] Tablets 1-22 contain "manifestations of the moon God Sin," including haloes around the moon, dates and duration of lunar visibility, and

the appearance of the "horns" of the lunar crescent. [52]
Tablets 23-37 relate to the Sun, and in particular, information regarding coronas, perihelia and eclipses.
The next series of tablets directs itself to natural phenomena, such as lightning, thunder, rainbows, cloud
formations, earthquakes and wind. Tablets 50/51 to
70 deal with planetary positions with respect to stars
or other planets, including first and last visibilities in
the morning, evening risings, and visually observable
features such as luminosity or color. Early apodoses
were concerned with state matters and natural disas-
ters, although by c. 700 BCE "nativity omens" gave
individual forecasts. [53] Some examples include,

> "If Venus stands in the crown of the Moon:
> the king's land will revolt against him." [54]

> "If Mars approaches the Scorpion: there will
> be a breach in the palace of the prince." [55]

> "If a child is born when Venus comes forth and
> Jupiter set, his wife will be stronger than he."

> "If a child is born when Mars comes forth
> and Jupiter set, the hand of his personal en-
> emy will capture him." [56]

As pointed out by the eminent Babylonian scholar Francesca Rochberg, it is particularly important for
modern sensibilities to apprehend that the "omens" of

the *Enuma Anu Enlil* were not mechanistic and did not mean that the "if-event" *caused* the "then-event." [57] Nor were omens "objects of worship." As Rochberg states, rather than a statement of causation, omens can be interpreted as: *"if" x, "expect also" y*. [58] She also describes omens as "verdicts," which under propitious circumstances (and using a contemporary metaphor) could be appealed to a higher court. The logic of these omens is similar to the modern astrological proposition that celestial and human occurrences correlate, indicate or are associated with one another. The difference between Babylonian and modern astrological constructs lies in the nature of their predicates. For us, the task starts and ends with attempting to ensure the accuracy of certain correlations. Ancient Babylonians began with the celestial canvas first, and only then attempted to discern the images, colors and patterns it displayed. The order of the cosmos was created and maintained divinely, which established the importance of its being examined and confirmed by direct astronomical observations. [59]

Astrology Benefitted from A Sophisticated Astronomical Knowledge Base

As should be apparent, ancient cosmologies were founded on an extraordinary level of acuity and sophistication, which interwove cosmological understanding, astronomical observation and astrological prediction. Many of us may have also been told that

Hipparchus of Rhodes (c. 127 BCE) "discovered" precession, or the "wobbling top" movement of celestial objects as seen from the perspective of Earth that is generally due to the tilt of the Earth's axis relative to its orbit. Recent archeo-astronomical discoveries have revealed that while our early ancestors may not have exactly known what caused precession, they were aware of its effects considerably before Hipparchus. [60] In contrast to this breadth of knowledge, I would warrant that not many of today's human beings have an inkling of precession or what it means.

Another example of this sophistication can be seen in early Mayan and Babylonian recognition of Venus' 8-year synodic cycle. In referring to the Babylonian *Venus Tablets of Ammisaduqa*, Nicholas Campion notes the "striking" nature of the conclusion that Venus returns to the exact position it held 8 years earlier. In order for ancient sky watchers to have appreciated this pattern, they would first have had to conclude that the same planetary body presented itself as a morning and an evening star. [61] The Mayans also demonstrated their continuing fealty to Venus, or Kukulcan, by orienting many structures at Chichen Itza to Venus' events. The Caracol tower (c 800 CE) is aligned to the Northern standstill of Venus. [62] The Governor's House at the Uxmal site lines up with the Southernmost standstill of Venus. As a final note, by 200—900 CE Mayan astronomers had not only developed a "recyclable" Venus calendar that was accurate to one day in 500 years and an eclipse warning table that still functions today, but they also generated a table noting Mars observations. As stated by archeo-astrologer Anthony Aveni, these efforts reflect the Mayan "fascination" with retrograde motion—another example of astronomical acumen. [63]

Astro-archeologist John Major Jenkins reveals the high level of sophistication in ancient astronomy by demonstrating that early Mesoamerican cosmologies were not static, but in fact changed as information cast new light on extant astronomical understandings. [64] The Olmec civilization (2,000 BCE—300 BCE) focused upon the stars of the polar region as its cosmic center. When their apprehension of precession challenged this worldview—again, an impressive feat in and of itself—another "cosmo-conception" arose, as seen in the Izapa (c. 500 BCE) culture. This organizing principle aligned itself with the zenith and the Sun's twice-yearly passage over the zenith at noon. Observers realized, however, that its predictions were latitude specific. By 200 BCE-50 CE, a third cosmic center was identified—the Pleiades. It is a pity that in the hubbub that surrounded speculations regarding a 12-12-12 doomsday, contemporary media missed the incredibly evocative and awe-inspiring Mayan recognition, as demonstrated at Chichen Itza (c. 600 CE, *et seq*), that on this date the Sun would align with the Galactic Center as well as the Pleiades.

A final example of the profundity of ancient astronomical knowledge can be found in the Incan apprehension of the *yana phuyu* or "black clouds" within the

Milky Way. [65] The brightness of the Milky Way is particularly prominent in the American tropics, and was perceived as the "umbilical cord that connected heaven and the underworld to the earth and the cosmic tree of life." [66] According to the Inca, the *yana phuyu* formed constellations whose contours were defined by animal shapes. [67] At the least, it is remarkable that the Inca identified dark clouds of interstellar matter as discrete entities. The insightful nature of this realization is also echoed in the modern concept of "negative space," which artists use to draw uneven, organic shapes. [Think of trying to draw strands of hair or each leaf on a tree. Instead of observing and then tracing the lines of the object, the artist looks at and draws the shape of the area that surrounds the object.] Apprehension of the "negative" space intrinsically reveals the "positive" space. The appreciation of "empty" space as an entity is remarkable, but even more importantly, also reflects an understanding that there is a larger unity that creates, maintains and embraces earth-sky realities.

While perhaps obvious, it is important to emphasize that not only was ancient astronomy highly developed, but astrology was as well. We are fortunately living in a time when English translations of many ancient astrological texts are becoming generally available, and they attest to this level of sophistication. Astrology was not "simply" divination—although I hasten to add that a modern aversion to such practices is unfounded. [68] Robert Hand makes a convincing point that since the Middle Ages and the

Renaissance, astrology has "de-volved" rather than evolved and only now is re-discovering itself. [69] The concept of self-actualization did not originate with contemporary self-help books, but instead finds its roots in the Greek philosopher Aristotle. He adds,

> "What I find really humorous . . . is that the most common allegation made about traditional astrology is that it is fatalistic and not oriented toward human potential. And I've actually found, from studying ancient philosophy as applied to astrology, that this philosophy gives the only system which has a solid philosophical rationale for human potential!" [70]

Sky Patterns Dwelled in All Levels of Ancient Society

It is difficult to apprehend how completely sky patterns and events permeated all areas of our forbears' lives. The connection was hand-in-glove, or "you can't have one without the other." [71] Prising them apart may appeal to contemporary sensibilities, but doing so obscures the bigger picture. Astrological significance did not arise from an arbitrary process. Celestial events were interwoven into every aspect of ancient lives and communities. Sky events were honored; stars and planets walked in tandem with human endeavors, informing and underlying all aspects of ancient society. The intricacy of these cosmological, astronomical and astrological connections demonstrates how the ancients came to know and name their celestial partners.

The intimacy of these connections is demonstrated by Stonehenge and other standing stone circles. These "henges" clearly served as celestial "timepieces" or "diagrams" designed to mark successive risings of the solstice Sun. [72] But their importance was far more profound. According to Anthony Aveni, "[f]or them, time was activity itself. It was lived rather than kept on a watch." [73] The circular structures also defined a physical location to which people could return. They provided security, a sense of regularity and the comfort of gathering in community. [74] In time, the stone circles represented religious or "sacred" observatories where the deities of the sky could take up their "assigned approximate places," in celebration of the entry of the sun god into the circular sanctuary. [75] The circle at Newgrange (2300 BCE) and the Maes Howe (2500 BCE) mound in Scotland in particular demonstrate this "numinous significance." Newgrange is designed so that once a year the light of the winter solstice sun enters an opening, or "roof box," directly above the main entrance, that only shines onto the floor of the inner sanctum. This light shines into the inner chamber—even after the entrance is completely blocked. [76] How amazing! In the 2,000 year period in which Stonehenge was used—a factor important in and of itself, its functions expanded to encompass a "cultic center, an economic center, a place of fortified habitations, a celestial temple and an observatory for tracking the sun and the moon—all at the same time." [77]

Although it is difficult to impart the full flavor here, Anthony Aveni describes the intricate sky-human marriage in the ancient Incan *ceque* system of city planning. [78] Maintaining order apparently constituted a touchstone of Incan culture. Their empire was circumscribed by the *Tahuantinsuyu* or "the Four Quarters of the Universe," which was subdivided into moieties delimiting the *Hanan*, or higher-ranking, up-river side of town and the *Hurin*, or the lower-ranking or down-river portion. This organization provided the organizing principle for sharing the precious waters of the Cuzco River. Superimposed on this pattern were 41 *ceques*, or "imaginary radial lines ... that cut across the landscape and were grouped like spokes on a wheel." [79] At the hub of this geographical wheel lay the Coriancha or the Temple of the Ancestors. Sight lines formed between Corinahca and pillars erected on the horizons allowed the Inca to note the passing of the Sun in mid-August, which in turn signaled the coming of the rains and the time for planting. The people within each *ceque* worshipped at shrines, or *huaca*, consonant with their social station, culminating with the Temple. Each element of this structure was designed to ensure the consonance of human and celestial order. The ceque system unified Incan ideas about kinship, geography, ideas about religion, social organization, calendar, astronomy and hydrology. [80]

The Erosion of Our Astrological Tradition—
The Unity of "As Above, So Below"

If there is one feature that stands out as distinguishing ancient astrology from that practiced today, it lies in the understanding of the inter-connecting unity of sky and human relations. In ancient cultures Sky bodies firmly dwelled within a cosmological unity, and although more powerful, they shared this unity with humanity. [81] Archeo-astronomer Giulio Magli describes this relationship as a "sacred landscape," whereby the, "[c]osmos gives order, and order transforms space into sacred space." [82] All was one; each was a piece in a series of "unfolding patterns." [83] The consonance of human and celestial cycles not only defined human existence and provided a sense of continuity, but constituted the physical manifestation of a more pervasive, underlying design and expression of cosmic intent. As described by Bernadette Brady, the cosmos was a ". . . ballet of co-creation between the divine and the rest of life, with the divine creating life and life creating the divine in a cyclic, never ending rhythm." [84] As Nicholas Campion states, "For pre-modern cultures, the cosmos was interior as much as exterior; it was inside us as much as outside us." [85] Brady provides an inspired description of humanity's role in the eternal and dynamic process of co-creating the cosmos,

"[The early] creation stories imply that we actually live inside creation and that we are a part of a relationship-rich pattern which is co-creating the web of life. Thus all of life, including humankind, has an important role to play in the co-creation of order and the health of one's environment. In these myths humans are not outside the system using the world like a construction site but rather we are inside the 'fish bowl' with the rest of life." [86]

It was as a result of this ancient cosmological understanding that planets were named. In playing their part on the celestial stage, planetary entities communicated their personalities to our forebears through the language of physical features, and celestial comings and goings. Because of the critical importance of these characteristics and occurrences, the ancients' observations of celestial features were no less empirically based than today's astronomical and computer-based calculations. Planetary names and identities, and the stories which came to embrace them, evolved from the studied accretion of these observations. Planetary legitimacy was not instantly conferred, nor dictated, but came about slowly, through consensus. And then stood the test of time.

In today's world, planets no longer breathe, lust, wage war, become jealous—or even do good deeds. Planets and stars lie in "outer space," separate and distinct from human activities. Critically, while many astrologers avow their intent to stem this tide of cosmological objectification, we may not fully appreciate that the predicate of an underlying, patterned intelligence no longer provides a justification for the *"As Above, So Below"* analogy that lies at the heart of ancient planetary nomenclature. [87] This oft-quoted concept was articulated in the Islamic text known as the *Emerald Tablet of Hermes* (c. 600/ 800 CE), but today's *"As Above, So Below"* incantation has been relegated to irrelevance and seems to constitute a hollow promise, a statement plucked from thin air. [88] The closest we come is to posit correlations and correspondences between discrete entities. Basket "A" is comprised of humans; Basket "B," celestials. Relationships are communicated by drawing lines or arrows between A-to-B lists of characteristics. When seen against this background, the *"As Above, So Below"* mantra may sound impressive, but what meaning does it really impart today? Just because we say it is so, doesn't make it so. Nor should we simply pull mythologically-derived names from our hats and instantly assign celestial bodies with corresponding mythologically-related qualities. Yet this is precisely what is occurring today.

The devolution of a unity paradigm has wrought profound changes for astrology and highlights why we now face the problem of naming proliferating celestial bodies. Our astro-"ology" now diminishes astrology's essential *raison d'etre*, and we simply do not notice the difference. Were it otherwise, we would be considering the question, for example—what is the meaning of adding something to a unity? Or, is there a model that might better accommodate the concept of astrological significance than that which we now use, which is to serially incorporate celestial entities *ad infinitem*? If, on the other hand, we continue to stand pat with the concept that planets and their respective energies denote discrete, if interacting, entities, then one or a hundred thousand more generate a traffic jam and not epistemological or cosmological anxiety. Of course, wholesale adoption of the ancient *zeitgeist* is ludicrous and likely a fool's errand. That is not the point. But given the crossroads at which we stand, it may be helpful to touch upon the strengths of astrology's underpinnings and harvest as many riches from this trove as we can. Just because contemporary society may shun aspects of pre-scientific paradigms should not allow us to shrink from this endeavor.

4

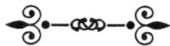

Some Details About Planetary Naming—From Classical Planets to Uranus and Neptune

We now turn from an analysis of astrology's roots or the *zeitgeist* that manifested the classical planets, to zeroing in on specific planetary names. It should be no surprise that the processes of naming the modern planets differ markedly from those of the classical planets, but many of us may not realize how pronounced and profound these differences are. As we will see, it is as if the flaws that crept into the process of designating the outer three planets intensified as more and more celestial bodies were "discovered."

How did the First Seven Classical Planets Get Their Names?

The names we now use for classical planets are largely drawn from early Greek and Roman designations, but the exact means by which the planetary identities were originally conceived is unknown. [89] Even NASA's website acknowledges they were discovered with a process "known by the ancients." [90] For the Greeks, the names were organized by combining such concepts as the four elements, the alternation of maleness and femaleness, and sign rulership based on the distance of the planets from the Sun. [91] While these delineations may seem familiar, and even convincing to Western ears, they also reflect the ancient Greek cultural proclivity to devise mathematical and philosophical categories. Seen in this light, the Greek descriptors reflect a process of incorporation and re-naming of previously existing planetary personalities and not an example of creation *ab initio*. [92] Carl Jung's description of archetypes as "archaic remnants" or "primordial images" fits exquisitely well in describing the development of our understanding of the Sun, the Moon, and the remaining classical planets. [93] The fact that cultures used different words for these archetypal images does not diminish the fact that their personalities came first and the names followed suit. As Carl Jung importunes, we should not confuse an archetype with the mythological symbols or "motifs" that are "nothing more than conscious representations." As he states in *Man and His Symbols*,

> "The archetype is a tendency to form such representations of a motif—representations that can vary in detail without losing their basic pattern." [94]

As every astrologer knows, lists of planetary associations that are regularly found in today's astrological how-to books never fully explain the elusive, ineffable quality that is the hallmark of an archetypal identity. Even so, these lists embody common threads of meaning that have coalesced and imparted planetary character over the centuries. We recognize the distinct qualities that "fit" with Mars, which fail to evoke the Moon or Jupiter. We appreciate qualities that connect the classical planets to a variety of human endeavors, including stages of life, mundane objects, plants, parts and diseases of the body, jobs or professions, animals, colors, metals and more. [95]

Planetary qualities are not only tied to written names (Sun, Moon, Mercury, etc.) but are richly and profoundly coupled with planetary glyphs. [96] The time-before-time quality of these glyphs is a clear testament to the legitimacy of their planetary counterparts. Each is deeply embedded in our psyche. While it is impossible to determine exactly when these symbols came to be known as we know them today, Irish astronomer and mathematician Annie Scott

Dill Maunder indicates, "as early as the 16th century, the planetary symbols were already stereotyped—not originated." [97] Horary astrologer Deborah Houlding states that by the 10th century a "full range of symbols was in frequent use." [98] Antecedents for the modern glyphs can also be seen in the Dendera Zodiac (1st century BCE) which was sculpted into the ceiling of the Temple of Hathor. [99] Glyphs also evoke esoteric principles that guided a number of spiritual perspectives, including the Chaldean or Neo-Babylonian (ca 600 BCE), Egyptian, Kabalistic (The *Zohar*) and early Christian and hermetic (*Hermes Trismegistus*) gnostics. [100] Although from ancient roots, these astrological glyphs retain their intuitive and mystical impact. It is no accident that many of us experienced the "aha" moment of a beginner's mind in apprehending the meaning of each classical planet when we saw the glyphs' line-up.

Classical Planets Stand the Test of Time

The following section summarizes the combination of key physical features and attendant personalities of each planet. I have also included references to the corresponding planetary glyphs as well as the fascinating correlations between alchemical metals and the chemical qualities "discovered" by modern science.

SUN—As its prodigious physical size imparts, the Sun anchors our "solar" system. As such, it represents the "big kahuna," bringing light, life, days, seasons, vital creativity—all of which define our Earthly experience. The Sun and solar energy symbolize our very existences.

GLYPH: Circle of Spirit. The central dot represents the manifestation point of solar creativity and/or the unfathomably intense. [101]

ALCHEMICAL METAL: Gold—the "noble" metal. It is the only metal that never tarnishes and needs to glitter in the Sun to express itself. [102]

MOON—The Moon bestows security and well-being by the regularity of her waxing and waning cycles of light. The rhythmic regularity of her cycles soothes our fears of change and the unknown. She can be recognized in the ebb and flow of tides. She signals when it is time to plant and when to harvest. Without food and water, even the Sun could not create human life. She acts as a cosmic "night light." With the courage of a mother, she endeavors to keep us safe by challenging the night's darkness. Both the luminaries (Sun and Moon) seem similar in size from our Earth-bound perspectives, but rather than projecting the egoic will of the Sun, the Moon welcomes our connection and ensures that it is safe to gaze upon her calm brilliance for as many moments as we choose.

GLYPH: Crescent of Soul. As a half circle, it connotes the reflective quality of the soul.

ALCHEMICAL METAL: Silver - has mirror-like or receptive qualities. It is the most lustrous or reflectant metal, requires darkness for chemical reactions and can be spoiled by exposure to daylight.

MERCURY—Shakespeare's King John recognizes the rapidity of Mercury's solar orbit when he asks his messengers to "Be Mercury, set feathers to thy heels, And fly like thought from them to me again." [103] Mercury's attention to details rather than the big picture is suggested by his relatively diminutive size. Mercury is the closest planet to the Sun, and the best time to see it is during fall morning and spring evening elongations. [104] These factors remind us that details and data can be easily swamped by bigger and perhaps more creative ideas. Mercury must dance around the Sun or be scorched. His eccentric orbit also evokes the intellect, difficult to pin down and nimbly flitting from one topic to another.

GLYPH: The Crescent of Soul on top of the Circle of Spirit, on top of the Cross of Matter. All 3 symbols are combined, with the spirit mediating between the soul and matter.

ALCHEMICAL METAL: Mercury or Quicksilver - its semi-liquid globules break apart and reform quickly. They resist containment, but different metals dissolved in Mercury can be easily amalgamated into other compounds.

VENUS—She—no doubt a "she"—is the brightest object in the sky aside from the Sun and Moon, and evokes love and beauty. Venus always rises and sets within three hours of the Sun, suggesting closeness to a male counterpart. Her movement is languid, like the caress of a besotted lover, such that Venus' day is longer than her year.

GLYPH: Circle of Spirit on Top of the Cross of Matter. The fact that spirit is above matter imbues the glyph with a sense of harmony, rather than implying that essential Feminine energy is limited to matters of the flesh or physicality.

ALCHEMICAL METAL: Copper - a soft and pliable metal that needs to be alloyed with other metals to attain strength. It has an aesthetic quality (versus iron/Mars). Electromagnetic current is made from the conductivity of copper and the ground of iron (Mars). Copper absorption is greater in women aged 20-59 than men. [105]

MARS—Mars is red but is icy cold as well, suggesting various stages of aggression and anger, as well as sexual passion. [106] Only Mercury has a planetary orbit that is more eccentric. This orbital pattern supports Mars' potential for independence, as well as rash irritability and recklessness. In contrast with Venus, Mars is cloudless, as if demonstrating his transparent and warrior-like willingness to go where others may fear to go. The fact that the Sun, Moon, Venus and Jupiter are all brighter than Mars may explain his competitive and energetic nature. Mars is also the first planet whose orbit lies outside that followed by Earth. Here again, we are reminded of an action-oriented hero, willing to "push the limits" and /or lead by sheer determination. With success, Mars comes to signify a type of purification of accomplishment, which astrologer Darby Costello has termed "*arête*" ["Ares"] or "excellence." [107]

GLYPH: Slanted Cross of Matter on top of Circle of Spirit. The fact the upper shape is an arrow rather than a complete cross adds exuberance to the symbol, and removes the potential for concluding that essential maleness is all about materiality overcoming spirit.

ALCHEMICAL METAL: Iron - it is the one metal that burns, is strong, useful. It makes blood red.

JUPITER—There are numerous features that emphasize Jupiter's expansiveness. He is so extensive that he maintains what may be described as his very own solar system, which includes four large and many smaller moons (50 confirmed and 17 provisional). As noted by NASA, Jupiter contains more than twice the amount of material of the other bodies orbiting our Sun. [108] One of Jupiter's companions, Ganymede, is the largest planetary moon (exceeds Mercury in diameter) and the only moon in the solar system known to have its own magnetic field. [109] The main or Galilean group of moons includes Io, Europa, Ganymede and Callisto. Each has "a distinctive world." NASA describes the orbits of Ganymede and Europa as a "tug-of-war," whereby Europa's orbital period is twice Io's. Perhaps Jupiter is aware of the maxim that it is best to keep one's friend close, but one's enemies even closer. Not to be outdone, Jupiter radiates more energy than he deigns to accept from another planetary companion, or rival, the Sun. He is a gas giant with his own magnetic field, who requires 12 Earth years to travel once around the zodiac. It is difficult to miss the impact of this largesse. These features emphasize Jupter's roles of Ruler and King; he can display lavish magnanimity and appreciation of higher order realities, as well as arrogant pretentiousness and being something of a blow-hard. His impressive size reminds us of the optimist, but also the optimism that may not be willing to accept the limitation of reality. The turbulence of Jupiterian surface storms and his Great Red Spot also remind us that his rages can be quite palpable. Our Earth could fit into this "Spot."

GLYPH: The Crescent of Soul Connected onto the Cross of Matter. The soul over matter connotes the "expansion of wisdom" or "unbinding the soul from matter." [110]

ALCHEMICAL METAL: Tin - a food preserver. When highly polished, it protects other metals from oxidation. It is malleable and does not tarnish.

SATURN—As the last planet regularly visible with the naked eye and one surrounded by clearly defined rings, Saturn reminds us of the unfortunate fact of limitation. We may attempt to avoid Saturn's cold hands, but Father Time will have his way in the end. His rings are strikingly beautiful, but the beauty lies in their perfection. This is the exquisite art of the printmaker or Japanese sumi-e painting, not the raucous beauty of paint globs slung onto canvas. His distance from the warmth of the Sun symbolically evokes existential fear and trepidation. Although Saturn's role as the farthest planet from the Sun has without question been supplanted—at least if you have a good set of binoculars or a telescope –having to work hard, face fears and rising above challenges still exist as familiar features of a Saturnian human experience.

GLYPH: The Cross of Matter on top of the Crescent of the Soul. It suggests "contraction through reality" or the soul seeking "right manifestation of it-self."[111]

ALCHEMICAL METAL: Lead - the "basest" of the metals. It was the first metal to be extracted from Earth. Lead is also a barrier to radioactive transmission and is the most stable metal. It is used in coffins, stored in bones, and is hard to get rid of. It is a heavy and dark metal, and is the slowest conductor and least lustrous or reflectant of the metals.

The Discovery of Uranus and Neptune

"O Romeo, O Romeo, wherefore art thou Romeo?
Deny thy father and refuse thy name ..."
[Shakespeare]

Uranus and Neptune were the first of the modern or "outer" planets to be discovered. Uranus was discovered in 1781 and Neptune in 1846. Astrologers have had far less experience with them than the classicals, although it is not clear that today's students of astrology are entirely aware of this distinction or the impact of assigning the stature of the Moon or Jupiter to Uranus and Neptune. Neither Uranus nor Neptune obtained their identities from centuries of observations, but came about as a result of scientific measurement and astronomical classification. This represents a significant departure from the invaluable test of time the classicals have been subjected to. The fact that their appearances resulted from better science does not contravene their existence, but it raises a cautionary flag. As we will see below, their names and associated identities surfaced as a result of confusing, haphazard and often parochial circumstances. These shortcomings insinuate some disturbing questions. Are astrologers going to glide by (read: ignore) these details? If we do so, what are we missing? Although one might say that the departure from the traditional naming process is well suited to Uranus' and Neptune's job descriptions, it is almost as if abiding by these designations involves first pinching one's nose to swallow a bitter pill. Swallow the pill we must, but the flaws in their naming processes urge us to cast about and further assess other bases for Uranus' and Neptune's significance. By doing so, we will discover interesting conclusions about the significations of the planets' discoveries in and of themselves. As an astrologer specializing in the history and philosophy of astrology, David McCann observes—perhaps the outer planets "could not be discovered until the world was ready for them." [112]

Uranus—Astronomical Discovery and Naming

Prior to its official discovery by Sir William Herschel on 13 March 1781, the planetary entity that came to be known as Uranus had actually been seen many times. [113] This said, the circumstances of its discovery are redolent with nationalistic undertones. It was initially named by Sir William Herschel as *Georgium Sidus* or "George's Star" in honor of his patron King George III. [114] As one might imagine and particularly outside of England, this name was not met with universal enthusiasm. During his reign King George had engaged in a number of military conflicts, including the American War of Independence and a variety of wars with Napoleonic France. The French astronomer Jerome Lalande proposed the name "Herschel." Neither side deterred, the British Royal Astronomical Society stuck with *"Georgium"* and, until 1813, the

French Bureau de Longitudes stayed with "Herschel." [115] During the period between its discovery and 1813, several other names were proffered, including Cybele (wife of Saturn), Astraea and Minerva. [116] The name "Neptune" was considered, although the fact that its name was meant to commemorate British naval victories in the American War of Independence rather than the god of the seas, underscores the patriotic fervor that surrounded the proposal. Johan Bode, a German astronomer argued for "Ouranos" or "Uranus" on the basis that just as Saturn was the father of Jupiter, the new planet should be named after the father of Saturn. His suggestion seems to represent an attempt to solve the controversy by choosing a less politically charged name. He explicitly pointed to the fact that "Uranus" replicated the kinds of names which had previously been used for planets, i.e. those with ancient Graeco-Roman origins. Bode ultimately won, although it took until 1850 for the British to concede. [117]

Uranus—Astrological Recognition and Confirmation of Significance

Contrary to the propensity of today's astrologers to rubber-stamp astronomically derived planetary names, astrologers who were presented with the new planet called Uranus did not instantly ratify its Uranian astrological significance. In fact, James Herschel Holden states that Uranus' discovery in 1781 did not initially attract much attention, and only some 30 to 50 years later did the "well known watercolorist" and astrologer John Varley (1778-1842) take note of it and try to establish its influence. [118] This apparent omission does not seem to reflect a lack of astrological interest in the new planet, but rather the relative paucity of publications about and interest in astrology during this time period. [119] Varley undertook a serious, scientific study of the events that Uranus seemed to provoke when it aspected other planets. As a result of this research, he noticed a pattern that if Uranus were excited by Mars, there would be "sudden or unexpected eruptions." In fact, one day after coming to this conclusion, Varley announced to his family that he had to stay at home because "something serious" was going to happen. At noon, his house caught on fire. As recounted by his son Albert, Varley refrained from picking up a bucket of water to staunch the flames, and instead,

> "He was so delighted at having discovered what the astrological significance of Uranus was, that he sat down while his house was burning, knowing though he did, that he was not insured for a penny, to write an account of his discovery." [120]

Exactly how or when Uranus came to be associated with Aquarius is also unclear, but it was certainly not instantaneous. Current scholarship indicates that the designation originated with Robert T. Cross, who wrote under the name of Raphael (1795-1832). [121] This conclusion did not obtain instant or universal acceptance, and over a century after its discovery, some astrologers dispute the attribution of Uranus' rulership to Aquarius. [122] Some accredit the rulership to John Varley (*A Treatise on Zodiacal Physiognomy*) published in 1828. The point here is that although we cannot be sure how Uranus came to join the astrological pantheon as it did, the astrological community not only took some time in assessing the new information, but attempted to use an astrological lens in doing so.

Neptune—Astronomical Discovery and Naming

Without a doubt, the naming of Neptune involved a turbulent process, [123] and reads something between a detective novel and a political free-for-all, replete with "unpardonable offenses in the eyes of a Frenchman" [124] and what appears to have been the deliberate "loss" of documents establishing British claims of first discovery.[125] An article tellingly entitled "The Case of the Pilfered Planet," refers to it as "Planetgate." [126] In preface to this drama, it was in fact Galileo who had first observed Neptune over 230 years earlier, but due to its proximity to Jupiter at the time, Galileo had concluded that it was a star. [127] The next step in Neptune's discovery came in the form of the Titius-Bode Law, publicized by Bode in 1772. This "Law" postulated a formulaic relationship between each planet's distance from the Sun. [128] In something of a foretaste of what became a vigorous battle for credit of discovery between French, British and, to a lesser degree, German astronomers, Jerome Leland (1795) and John Herschel (1830) also observed Neptune, but did not realize what they were seeing. [129] A more concerted search for the planetary body was launched in 1821 when the French mathematician Alexis Bouvard speculated that the gravitational pull of something rather large had to be causing Uranus to deviate from its predicted orbit. Astronomical consensus was soon reached that this perturbation was caused by another planet, and armed with Titius-Bode's mathematical predictions, the hunt was on. As an interesting detail, the search for the unknown planet was complicated by the fact that the mathematics presented an "inverse problem"—rather than accounting for perturbations by known planetary positions, in this case the problem was how to determine the position of an unknown planet that exerted its own gravitational force. [130]

At this point, accounts of Neptune's "discovery" diverge, largely between French and British versions. The flavor of this divergence is not only apparent in the vigorous efforts to obtain official astronomical recognition, but it also surfaces in the more than uncomplimentary descriptions the astronomical participants (and their respective champions) used to describe their competitors. We begin the story in 1841, when halfway through his undergraduate education, University of Cambridge mathematician John Couch Adams came across Cambridge Royal Observatory Director and University Professor James Challis' 1832 paper "Report on the Progress of Astronomy" while browsing in a Cambridge bookstore. [131] Adams has been described as having "brilliantly" obtained his mathematics degree from Cambridge (1843) [132] and was an early prodigy, but was also "a shy and callow youth" [133] who would probably be seen today as having Asperger's Syndrome. [134] (We can easily perceive which is the English version versus the French.) Regardless, Adams was intrigued and began to work on the problem of the unknown planet. By 18 September 1845, he believed he had deduced the planet's position and took this news to Professor Challis. Challis, in turn, attempted to connect him to George Biddell Airy, the Astronomer Royal and Director of the Royal Observatory in Greenwich, in order to determine how to disseminate his discovery. Airy has been portrayed as a "first class organizer . . . [who] had restored the Observatory's reputation," but was also a man "obsess[ed] with 'order and method," loathe to taking advice from others and slow to change his mind "even when it had become fairly clear that he was in the wrong." [135] (Again, we can see the stark differences in these descriptions.)

Airy's proclivity to maintain "order" apparently extended to his personal schedule as well. This leads us to the infamous non-meeting of Adams and Airy. It appears that on 21 October 1845 Adams called on

Airy at his home in Greenwich Hill, but Airy refused to see him (probably twice). Failing to meet Airy directly, Adams claimed that he left a note with Airy's butler setting forth his computations to date. Airy subsequently claimed not to have received this note. This missed connection remains a source of much controversy. In assessing exactly what took place, for example, did Airy refuse to see Adams because it would interrupt his schedule? Was Airy at his residence when Adams called? Did Adams actually leave a note that Airy failed to publish? Was it the Airy butler who failed to deliver this note? Or, had Airy just returned from a trip and was understandably fatigued? [136] In any event, on 5 November, Airy wrote Adams, requesting more specific information about his computations as to the Uranian perturbations that located the position of the new planetary body. [137] Airy's request has been characterized as "essentially irrelevant" and "trivial." [138] However, modern scholarship contends that Airy's request was entirely appropriate because astronomers needed actual or heliocentric information about a planet's orbit, not just a mean or average orbit. [139] Regardless, Adams did not respond to Astronomer Royal Airy's request. And thus another layer of confusion began: was this lack of response due to the fact that Adams had been rebuffed or because he knew his calculations needed more work? [140]

Time passed, and in June 1846, Airy received information that a French mathematician Urbain

Le Verrier had pegged a planetary body in much the same manner as Adams. He thereupon wrote to Le Verrier asking for the same type of data he had requested from Adams, but intriguingly, made no mention whatsoever of Adams or his computations. On 13 July, Airy tasked Challis to direct his telescope to the area predicted by Adams. Challis agreed, but the enthusiasm and astronomical acumen with which he undertook this charge has been seriously questioned. English astronomer and author Patrick Moore in particular takes Challis to task, stating, "Even if Airy had been dilatory, Challis, in the end, was even more so." [141] Challis has also been characterized as an "incompetent bumbler." [142] These charges arise from claims that Challis took six weeks to carry out Airy's instructions and he should have used a telescope with a more powerful eyepiece. [143] To his chagrin, Challis subsequently realized that he had observed "Neptune" on 29 and 30 July and 4 August, 1846. The Challis defense seems to be that he did not have sufficient maps in time to locate the planetary body any earlier. [144] No one appears to have escaped the Neptune saga unscathed!

On 13 November 1846, Airy publicly announced Adams 1845 "predictions" at a Royal Observatory meeting, but this timing undoubtedly related to the French pursuit of the planetary body that was perturbing Uranus' orbit. If events in England had been somewhat checkered and confusing, at this point the Neptune controversy deepened over exactly who, representing which country, became aware of what - when. To understand the nature of the controversy, we need to return to 22 September 1845, when Francois Arago, the Director of the Paris Observatory, tasked Observatory colleague and well-respected mathematician Urbain Jean Joseph Le Verrier to follow up on the unknown planet. [145] Lest we think that the socially inept Adams, the arrogant Airy or the bumbling Challis are the only participants in the search for "Neptune" who have been singled out as objects of criticism, Le Verrier has been described as being "brash and abrasive," "autocratic," a "difficult personality," and something of a manipulator. [146] To return to substance, however, on 1 June 1846, Le Verrier presented preliminary conclusions to the Paris Observatory regarding his method for locating the planet that eventually became known as Neptune, as well as its approximate position. [147] By 26 June, Airy requested clarification of this information, and by 28 June, Le Verrier responded, requesting that Airy return the favor and provide him with any corrections he might have. Airy did not respond.

On 31 August, Le Verrier published what he believed to be a precise position for the planet. Unfortunately, the French astronomical community's response to Le Verrier's computations was as "lackluster" as Professor Challis had been to Adams' mathematics and Royal Astronomer Airy's instructions. [148] Thus "disillusioned," on 18 September, Le Verrier asked Johan Gottfried Galle of the Berlin Observatory to train its telescope in the direction that Le Verrier had suggested. Luckily for Le Verrier, "Galle was no Challis." [149] On the night of 23-24 September 1846, Galle sighted the planet, and shortly thereafter Le Verrier and several other astronomers confirmed the sighting. Believing that he had therefore earned naming rights, on 25 September, Galle wrote Le Verrier proposing the name "Janus." Janus is the Roman god of beginnings and endings, as well as doors, gates and passageways. He is also often depicted as having two faces that look out in opposite directions, where one face looks to the future and the other to the past. Galle chose "Janus" because this "double face signifie[d] its position at the frontier of the solar system." [150]

In a tone which reflects the increasing tumult, and although he had received Galle's letter on 28 September, on 30 September Le Verrier chose to announce "his" discovery of the new planetary body in two French newspapers (*National* and *Journal des Debats*). Le Verrier also took it upon himself to propose that it should be named "Neptune," and also identified the planet's symbol—the trident. On 1 October, Le Verrier wrote three European observatories advising of his choice of "Neptune," claiming "rather strangely" that the Bureau des Longitudes had already given its consent to the name—which was not the case and, about which claim, litigation almost ensued. [151] Le Verrier made a formal announcement of his discovery to a "packed" meeting of the Academie des Sciences on 5 October. At this meeting Le Verrier's friend and enthusiastic supporter Francois Arago (the Director of the Paris Observatory who had initially tasked Le Verrier with the project) dramatically pledged that he would never name the planet anything other than the "*Planete de Le Verrier.*" A few months later the Academie adopted a symbol for the new planet which tellingly combined an "L" and a "V." [152] The French press fanned the public's ecstatic applause for their countryman's discovery.

Back in England, the "discovery" of Neptune by either Le Verrier or Galle was beginning to cause a stir. Royal Astronomer Airy learned of it when visiting a Denmark observatory, but he did not immediately issue public comment. English mathematician and astronomer, and son of William Herschel, Sir John Herschel was apparently the first to publicly break the news of the French discovery, but at the same time rather cagily referred to Adams' conclusions. [153] On 14 October, "in a rather transparent effort to pour oil on potentially troubled waters," Airy took something of the same tone, writing Le Verrier and congratulating him on his discovery, while at the same time referring to certain "English investigations." [154] On 14 October 1846, Challis and Adams presented an article to *The Athenaeum*, which was published on 17 October, proposing the name "Oceanus." By doing so, they decisively placed their oar in the water of the growing international contest for naming rights. Debates began to rage and dueling cartoons abounded in the public press, with the British siding with Adams and "Oceanus", and the French with Le Verrier and "Neptune." In a "stormy" meeting of the Academy of Sciences in Paris on 19 October, Arago staunchly defended Le Verrier (both the mathematician and the planetary name), and characterized the British findings as "*clandestin*" (clandestine) and a "*pretention*" (pretentious exaggeration). [155] The English response came in the form of Airy's 13 November announcement at the Royal Observatory meeting in which Adams 1845 "predictions," referred to above, were presented.

Forgetting for a moment the English-French furor, there was, however, still the matter of Galle. The French summarily dismissed his claims on the basis that his letter of September 25 had only claimed he had "found" the planet and not "discovered" it. The German press acclaimed Galle's triumph, but it was to no avail. Le Verrier wrote Airy, Galle and other astronomers, indicating his rejection of "Janus" as it might erroneously infer that it was the last planet in the solar system. It also appears that Le Verrier, or his representatives, did some informal but obviously effective politicking with Johann Franz Encke, Director of the Berlin Observatory and Galle's boss.

By this point in latter 1846, Le Verrier acknowledged the valiant defense mounted by his boss Arago, asserting that other claims of priority had besmirched his honor. He found himself, however, in something of a "Hamlet-like" pickle—go along with Arago's seemingly impetuous, but quite complimentary, proffer of "Le Verrier," or stick with "Neptune," the name Le Verrier himself had initially proposed. [156] The debate was also causing so much turmoil within the astronomical community that it became clear that Le Verrier might stand a chance of losing all naming rights. Up to this point, he had not publicly acknowledged the "Le Verrier" planetary name. In what seems to be a not too subtle attempt to entice Sir John Herschel to throw his weight to his cause, Le Verrier wrote to Herschel on 28 November, indicating that he would rather have Uranus named "Herschel," in honor of John's father William. Le Verrier signed the letter "U J Le Verrier and Mr. Thomas of Hell No 5." [157] It is also interesting to note that in a memorandum that Le Verrier enclosed with his letter, he used the name "Herschel" in lieu of "Uranus" only once—the title page, while the text of the memorandum referred to "Uranus." Although likely unmoved by this inducement but perhaps attempting to promote compromise regarding the escalating controversy, in early 1847, Sir John suggested alternate names: "Demogorgon," "Minerva," and "Hyperion" the "transcender." [158] In his own version of tit-for-tat, however, Sir John not only referred to Hyperion's role as a "transcender," but a "son of Uranus and Terra . . . the inhabitants of *terra* having come to its knowledge by means of Uranus." Uranus, of course, had been discovered by his father, William Herschel. The astronomical back-and-forth between England and

France regarding naming rights was also no doubt fueled by the larger political strains between England and France, but on 28 February 1847 Airy wrote Le Verrier in what seemed to represent an effort to extend an olive branch. In his letter Airy indicated a willingness to support "Neptune," which was, of course, the name Le Verrier had initially proposed. Unfortunately, he also not too subtly pointed out that "the decision of a Deputy [Arago] is far less binding than that of the original discoverer [Le Verrier]." [159] Le Verrier took offense at this rather "indelicate" comment about his principal defender—Arago, and hence Airy committed an "unpardonable offense" in the "eyes of a Frenchman." [160] Airy was forced to publish a formal apology in the *Atheneaum*, although his private correspondence maintained that Arago had "done grievously wrong ... with a sort of craftiness entirely setting aside common rules of propriety." [161]

The intrigue was not, however, entirely over. For many years, the British version held sway. Charges were also made against Adams and Challis that they had either hidden or forged the papers that supported their claims of discovery. In response, the Greenwich Royal Observatory claimed that the underlying documentation was unfortunately "unavailable." [162] In 1998, however, the "Neptune file" of correspondence related to the planet's discovery which had been "missing" from the Observatory, appeared in Chile. They were found in the papers of Olin J. Eggen, who had served as chief assistant to the Astronomer Royal and had ostensibly "borrowed" the papers to write biographies of Airy and Challis. He had previously denied having the files. These papers included Adams' series of computations. Recent scholarship reflects that on 13 November, 1845, Adams began a letter responding to Airy's request regarding the hypothetical planet's orbit, but failed to complete it. This failure, it is argued, represents a tacit acceptance that he had not predicted Neptune's orbit with the precision that was necessary for astronomical observation.

In a final ironic twist, it also appears that neither Adams nor Le Verrier accurately predicted the position of Neptune, greatly overestimating the planet's actual distance from the Sun. [163] Lest an American audience believe that it was entirely removed from the fray, on 9 February 1847, Sears Cook Walker, an astronomer at the US Naval Observatory, published his computations regarding Neptune, which substantially differed from Le Verrier's. Anxious to burnish the reputation of the nascent American academic astronomical community, the self-educated mathematician and Harvard University Perkins Professor of Mathematics and Astronomy Benjamin Pierce confirmed Walker's calculations and quite publicly announced that, given Le Verrier's errors, Galle's observation was only a "happy accident." Some American astronomers were taken aback at this seeming intrusion, while others "applauded Peirce's efforts in defense of American astronomers who [had] been passed over in silence, or met with sneers instead of arguments." As might be expected, the Royal Astronomical Society expressed its vigorous displeasure with Pierce's claims, and Le Verrier wrote a "scathing" letter to the *National Intelligencer* in Washington, DC.

In the end, it must be said that the mathematicians and astronomers from England and France, as well as those in Germany and the United States, relied on each other's data. One wonders, however, whether Sherlock Holmes or Inspector Hercule Poirot should have been consulted at the outset!

Neptune—Astrological Recognition and Confirmation of Significance

As with Uranus, other than the obvious Graeco-Roman mythological connections, there is a marked paucity of information about how Neptune came to obtain its astrological identity. James Herschel Holden claims that the designation was made in the 1890's, some 50 years after the planet Neptune's discovery. [164] In 1929, Scottish astrologer Maurice Wemyss (1892-1973) linked Neptune with Libra, as well as Uranus to Scorpio and "the asteroids as a group" to Pisces. [165] As was the case with Uranus, it is important to reiterate that the lack of contemporaneously published information regarding this process may not reflect the astrological community's lack of interest in Neptune, but the rather scattered nature of the astrological community. While today's tendency of astrologers to defer to astronomical nomenclature when conferring astrological significance to new celestial bodies may have its roots in what may seem a rather complacent attitude towards Uranus' and Neptune's identities, I believe we need to give the earlier astrologers the benefit of the doubt. They were dealing with entirely new circumstances. Today's astrologers cannot rest on the laurels of this explanation.

A First Take-Away Message Regarding the Naming of Uranus and Neptune

What can we glean from the processes surrounding the naming of Uranus and Neptune? The following ideas extrapolate some common themes, and at least insofar as providing substance to choice of the names "Uranus" and "Neptune," they do not paint a very positive picture:

1. Individuals rather than communities or the collective chose the names.
2. The names that were chosen reflect the overt ethnocentrism, eccentricities and biases of the namers.
3. The planetary namers were astronomers and mathematicians.
4. There was no astrological input, nor was astrological input considered relevant.
5. In comparison to the classical planets, the process of naming was accomplished with lightning speed.

6. The names came first, and attendant meanings second. This cart-before-the-horse feature of the naming process delegated the ascription of astrological significance to a *post hoc* circumstance.

7. Astrologers kept quiet and did business as usual.

Do Physical Features Tie Uranus and Neptune to Their Names?

As we have seen when examining the ancient roots of astrology, keen observation of celestial features and events formed the basis of classical planetary names. A number of physical features of Uranus and Neptune also correlate to their astrological meanings or keywords. It is important to recognize, however, that these associations are not as numerous or firmly grounded as the first seven planets. It is as if when the modern planets emerged, there was a slight lifting off or buoyance from the structure that embodied classical planetary naming. This movement conjures an image of a space station slowly un-docking from its homeport as it ventures into the vast, quiet universe. By the time we reach the newer celestial entities, however, our space station is zooming ahead. It is also important to recognize that however correlative certain physical features are to Uranus' and Neptune's astrological significance, the designations came first and the rationales second. They serve more as corroborative, rather than dispositive, factors.

Certain physical features undeniably correlate with Uranus' planetary personality. Philip Sedgwick states that Uranus "seems to be the perfect planet for upsetting the apple cart of the outer limit of the solar system." [166] That said, contemporary astronomy has moved past attempting to delineate any definitive limits to the solar system. Instead, today's astronomers characterize the end of the solar system as an amorphous "depletion zone" at the edge of the Sun's magnetic reach. [167] On a humorous note, perhaps Uranus is the gift that keeps on giving! [168] In any event, the astrological qualities of individuality and unconventionality correlate well with its orbital eccentricity and perpendicularity. [169] [170] Uranus' north-south axis actually tilts some 99° from the Sun, and its equator therefore lies almost perpendicular to the plane of the solar system. [171] This obliquity results in the sideways quality of Uranus' orbit, as well as an irregular magnetic field that is tilted nearly 60° from its axis of rotation and offset from the center of the planet by one-third of its radius. Uranus is also one of the three planetary bodies in our solar system which rotates East to West. (The other is Venus; and the dwarf planet Pluto). These factors underscore the Uranian capacity to march into corners when it may be socially unacceptable or seemingly extreme to do so, and if necessary, advocate for these ideas—even to the extent of challenging solar order. Its unusual orbital tilt also means that unlike the other gas giants, Uranus lacks any real internal heat source. This quality correlates with a certain cold intellectuality or the capacity for visionary genius that Uranus is known for, and suggests its designation as a higher octave of Mercury. On the other hand, Uranus' absorption of solar energy, as opposed to its radiation, does not necessarily correlate with its role as a rule-buster. Rather than exerting independence or pushing its agenda forward, it is incorporating energy from the power structure—the Sun. From Earth, Uranus' surface seems almost seamlessly smooth. Like Saturn, it has a system of rings, although they are less dense. Uranus has at least two sets of 27 Moons, although none are particularly large. While these factors suggest a certain fraternity with Uranus' planetary companions rather than the rebellious, go-it-alone quality Uranus is known for, they do not seem to militate strongly for or against the name given to Uranus.

The correlation between physical features and astrological significance seems less strong with Neptune than Uranus. If there is one feature, however, that most clearly evokes Neptune's astrological personality, it is the roundness or lack of eccentricity of its solar orbit, a close second to Venus. Its proximity to an almost perfectly circular orbit also evokes the intrinsic beauty and harmony of Venus, as well as a Neptunian yearning for subjective one-ness and "consciousness itself." [172] Neptune is also considered a higher octave of Venus, which highlights this correlation. [173] Due to atmospheric methane, both Neptune and Uranus appear blue. As a result, Neptune cannot claim sole ownership of oceanic coloration. Of the Jovian planets, Neptune is also the most dense. [Saturn is the least dense, with Jupiter and Uranus similarly dense]. [174] This quality does not necessarily align well with Neptune, although it is certainly not formed of the rock and solid materials common to the terrestrial planets. Although Neptune is the farthest planet from the Sun [Pluto is a dwarf planet and spends 20 years of its 248-year solar circumference within Neptune's orbit.], it generates enough internal energy to "drive the fastest planetary winds seen in the solar system." [175] These storms are three times stronger than Jupiter's and nine times stronger than Earth's. In fact, both Neptune and Jupiter exhibit storms that have coalesced into single large systems. The super-intense storm activity on Neptune is known as the "Great Dark Spot," whereas Jupiter's is the "Great Red Spot." Neptune's Great Dark Spot is also large enough to contain the entire Earth. Although not as pronounced, the irregularity of Neptune's magnetic field is similar to Uranus due to the tilt of its rotational axis [46° as opposed to 60°], although its axis is even farther off center than Uranus [one half of a radius from the center]. [176] This Neptunian off-kilter storminess evokes the tumultuous nature of waves and the ups and downs of "Neptunian trends ... that creep up on us from a feeling level." [177] It does not correspond quite as well to Neptune's ego-merging or ineffable nature. Due to its distance from the Sun, Neptune's atmosphere is a "frigid -225ºC (373ºF)." [178] Neptune also sports rings, which were initially thought to be arcs or incomplete circles, and a number of moons that have largely been named after sea nymphs. Other planets also exhibit rings (i.e. Saturn, Jupiter) and moons (i.e. Earth, Jupiter). The sea nymph nomenclature came after Neptune's designation. These features do not provide independent support for Neptune's astrological identity.

Glyphs in the style of those adopted for the classical planets have, of course, been assigned to both Uranus and Neptune. Uranus' glyph has been described as a "Cross of Matter between two Crescents of Soul and on top of Circle of Spirit. [179] Neptune's glyph looks like a trident and represents the "Crescent of Soul encompassing an upward-extending Cross of Matter." These glyphs were, however, chosen after the planetary names for Uranus and Neptune were selected, which was not the case with the classical planets. As such, these glyphs were not formulated as a result of consensus reached through millennia of planetary and collective experience. These glyphs may accurately and profoundly describe Uranian and Neptunian attributes, but they do not deliver the same kind of justification or validation that the glyphs provided the classical planets.

An Astrological Mismatch Between
Identity and Meaning

Aside from the uncomfortable questions posed by the haphazard nature of Uranus' and Neptune's naming processes, as well as the less than satisfying confirmation from their physical features, there is an additional area of concern and it arises more from astrological than astronomical or mythological considerations. This difficulty relates to the stark dissonance that exists between the ethnocentric and personality-driven nature of the naming processes and the astrological significations that ultimately came to evoke Uranus and Neptune. These planets are generally characterized as universal, collective, generational phenomena. They are often accompanied with words such as "underlying pattern," "transcendence," "over-arching," and "transpersonal." The fact that these descriptions have supposedly arisen because of Uranus' and Neptune's greater distance from Earth, as opposed to the "personal" or "social" planets, fails to adequately address the juxtaposition between their astrological significance and the "me first" or "my country first" parochial interests that lie at the heart of their naming. These differences are so striking as to represent opposite ends of a spectrum. We have, on the one hand, classical planets that purportedly describe personal characteristics that coalesced as a result of an accretion of collective wisdom, and on the other, we have two outer planets that correlate with universal astrological meaning but were individually and parochially designated. This juxtaposition is troubling and invites further investigation.

What Difference Does All This Make?

If we conclude that as a result of flawed naming processes, the planets we know as Uranus and Neptune cannot unequivocally claim their places in the Roman pantheon, then where and how do we proceed? As earlier stated, it is as if a slight deviation is in the wind—away from the classical structure, a hint of changes to come, but certainly not a total wrenching away. Importantly, were we to categorically reject these planets on the basis that they cannot claim legitimacy from age-old processes or that they do not look or act like classical planets, we would be precipitously closing the book on any future celestial discoveries and crystallizing the vibrancy of astrological knowledge. That is not a positive course, and not simply because Uranus and Neptune are big planets, as opposed to dwarf planets or asteroids. Today's astrology demonstrates that the astrological significance accorded them fits, and they have in fact "worked" for one and a half to two centuries. This evidence cannot and should not be casually dismissed. We must then pose some questions. Does any consonance between these planets' physical features and their identities provide sufficient legitimacy? Or, is there a heretofore undiscovered blueprint for ascertaining astrological significance? *Importantly, does the nature of the naming process in and of itself—as opposed to the details of its designation—tell us something? It does.*

The Medium Is the Message—Global Movements Establish Identity

At least one answer to these questions lies in the remarkable nexus between (1) the discoveries of Uranus and Neptune and (2) the manifestation of global events and movements. As will shortly be described more fully below, these event clusters provoked paradigm shifts that broke up the status quo (Uranus) and exposed the world to different visions (Neptune) of how lives could be lived. Because the consonances between these events and planetary identities seem so much more persuasive than correlations predicated upon the basis of physical feature resemblances, I propose that the occurrences of these events rather than their physical features legitimize their names and attendant astrological significance. This proposition is not the same as noting mundane astrological correspondences, although the insights of this branch of astrology are highly relevant in identifying the type of events and movements that are associated with these planets. As we will see below, mundane analyses amplify rather than detract from my proposition.

Perhaps the best example of the seminal events and movements that provide astrological significance to Uranus and Neptune is the fact that they were officially identified when they were. They were the first planets to blast or sail into our view for millennia,[180] and have unquestionably triggered profoundly new understandings about the nature of humanity and the cosmos. There is an additional nuance to the timing of Uranus and Neptune's appearances that is subtle, but uniquely relevant. While most of us speak of the "discoveries" of Uranus and Neptune, it is more accurate to describe their appearances as reflecting an expansion of *human awareness*. These planets have obviously been around for quite some time, but at least metaphorically, it is human awareness that brought them identity and meaning. To be sure, the classical planets have also existed for billions of years, but we have been aware of them since the dawn of our conscious existence. To the extent that it is human awareness that midwifed the birth of the modern planets, the cosmos seems to be directing its laser pointer to the part of the lesson that relates to humanity and the Earth we occupy. This cosmological frame of reference, as well as the need for us to attend to our new awareness, is Earth or terra-centric.

Other resonances that support Uranus and Neptune's astrological significance generally include the following:

Uranus (1781)—A most salient correlation between the discovery of Uranus and significant world events exists with the discovery of uranium by the German chemist Martin Heinrich Klaproth in 1789. [181] Uranium has the unique property of being the

"only naturally occurring fissile isotope," and the sub-
sequent medical and military uses spawned by its discovery are obvious. [182] Although the first atomic bomb
tests were not conducted until the 1940s (closer to
the discovery of Pluto in 1930), the Industrial, French
and American Revolutions also took place during this
period. These events toppled the economic, social and
political *status quo*. Social betterment and the extension of political involvement—life, liberty and the
pursuit of happiness or *liberté, egalité, fraternité*—were
touchstones of these movements. As also stated by astrologer and author Steven Forrest, these movements
stressed the "dignity of the individual and his right to
question authority." [183] History is, of course, replete
with one country or culture conquering another or ac-
quiring territory, but these movements represented a
fundamental re-structuring and reorientation to personal freedom and autonomy that spanned the world.
On the other hand, the first execution by guillotine
was in 1792, and social upheaval undeniably accompanied the positive aspects of these revolutions. [184] We
might also take note of the publication of *A New and
Complete Illustration of the Celestial Science of Astrology*
(1784-1788) by Freeman Ebenezer Sibly. As acknowledged by Nicholas Campion, before this publication
the practice of astrology had largely been relegated to
"almanac readers and the clients of fortune-tellers." [185]
Sibly's "extensive and detailed account of astrology"
reversed this trend. Interestingly, the Siblys were also
religious nonconformists and "political radicals in the

populist tradition ... who enthusiastically supported the rebels in the American War of Independence ... and were keen to disseminate knowledge among the masses." [186] This quotation could easily fit in a list of Uranian characteristics.

Mundane astrology provides additional confirmation to the ties between Uranus and tradition-breaking world events. [187] The astrologer, historian and philosopher David McCann points out that on 13 March 1781 when William Herschel first sighted Uranus, the chart displayed a "striking" T-square involving Uranus in Gemini in the 8th House opposite Mars conjunct with Saturn in Sagittarius, squared by the Sun in Pisces. [188] The Moon, Venus and Mercury were also unaspected. McCann reads the mundane chart as "the nativity for the age of scientism: the intellect (Uranus in Gemini) without feelings (Moon and Venus) or reason (Mercury) compounded with arrogance (Saturn-Mars-Uranus.)" He also calls our attention to the correlation between Uranus and aviation. The Montgolfier brothers launched their hot air balloons in 1783, "with Uranus transiting the square of radical Mercury." Astrologer Kelly Lee Phipps notes the 1760 ingress of Uranus into Aries that portended the beginning of a pioneering and revolutionary phase of development. [189]

Astrologer and author Gary Caton uses a classical approach for his mundane analysis and initially points out that due to the Scorpio Ascendant and Uranus' placement in the 8th house, it might initially seem as if we were looking at a chart more befitting the discovery of Pluto. [190] Given the Scorpio Ascendant, Mars is the Chart Ruler or the Domicile Lord (defined as: the one who gives the objects of the house where it is located) of the Uranus discovery chart and lies in the 2nd house, Sagittarius (fire). Mars also conjoins the star Aculeus, one of two stingers constituting the tail of the constellation Scorpius (the other is Acumen). [191] In characterizing this Mars as a "dubious giver," Caton states "the planet that gives in this chart is a fire sign and on the sting of the Scorpion—sounds kind of like the gifts of the fire-breathing dragon of the nuclear age." The opposing connection between Mars in the 2nd and Uranus in the 8th house underscore 8th house qualities of "loss, anxiety, decay and death." This sounds a great deal like the Atomic Age. Uranus is also visually located between the two horn stars of Taurus, which suggests it has "caught the proverbial bull by the horns." [192] Uranus may also find itself in the "horns" of a dilemma—whether to use the newfound knowledge it generated to positive or more nefarious ends. Caton also finds the "double-edged sword" nature of modern technology in Venus' placement. Venus is the Debility Lord (one who takes away things of the house where it is located) and lies in the 5th house (Joy), Pisces (exaltation). As such, she can give prosperity and health to a nation or people, as well as take it away. Caton correlates this placement with the modern conveniences that are correlated with Uranus' discovery, that have made life "easier and more pleasurable, especially for the privileged, [while] on the other hand it has eroded the values and very fabric of society."[193]

Neptune (1846)—As might be expected, the global events and movements associated with Neptune are more diffuse, although no less significant. It was at this time that Romanticism was evident in a variety of areas. This was a broad-based and profound movement that espoused changing from a model of objectivity and scientism to emotion and aestheticism. As Nicholas Campion describes,

> "The Romantics were driven by nostalgia for a lost paradise in which humanity and cosmos were one. The main vehicle by which the anguish of loss might be assuaged, and the truth of the spirit in nature and the universe revealed was the man of genius, the artist or poet. Yet we shouldn't imagine that the Romantics necessarily stood in a state of opposition to everything the Enlightenment thinkers believed in. They reacted against Newtoniansm, but only in its materialist, mechanical form. Convinced that the universe defied scientific explanation, the Romantics instead sought to restore spirit and soul to it, to re-enchant it . . . ."[194]

These descriptions sound as if they have come straight out of an astrology textbook on the significance of Neptune. Or, as stated by poet and critic Charles Baudelaire in 1846,

> "Romanticism is precisely situated neither in choice of subject nor in exact truth, but in a way of feeling." [195]

This time period also saw the opening up or—as seen through different eyes—the erosion, of societal structures and values. Significant humanitarian efforts were undertaken, including the increasing recognition of racial inequalities which led at least in part to the American Civil War (attack on Fort Sumter in April 1861), promulgation of child labor laws, emancipation of serfs, the growth of public schools, and the founding of the Red Cross and the Salvation Army. Victor Hugo exemplifies this spirit with the passionate social conscience he articulated in *Notre-Dame de Paris*, known in English as The Hunchback of Notre-Dame (1831) and *Les Misérables* (1862). The first Women's Rights Convention took place in Seneca Falls in 1848, and in the same year Karl Marx and Freidrich Engels published *The Communist Manifesto* which offered a utopian solution to economic oppression and class struggles. In 1848, "the people" revolted against European monarchies. [196] While these events can be characterized as positive forces for social change, they also contained seeds for overuse and addiction. However altruistic the idea of communism was, its virtual canonization led to great suffering. The ills arising from the promise of Industrial Revolution and capitalism also began to surface, including increasingly unregulated economic growth leading to divisions between the very rich and poor, materialism and mass consumption. The petroleum industry also began during this period (1859), which has led to a decidedly unhealthy addiction to oil. In an interesting correlation with Neptune's reputation with dreaminess and drugs, the first public demonstration of using ether to anaesthetize surgical patients took place less than a month after the discovery of Neptune. [197] Prior to this time, surgical procedures were largely unavailable, little was known about how to prevent infection and, other than tourniquets and physical restraints, not much was available to reduce surgical pain. [198] On the other hand, over-use of medications brings its own set of problems.

Interestingly, Neptune's appearance also correlates with the rise of spiritualism in the West. Here too, we can see the positive and negative faces of Neptune. As noted by Steven Forrest, Neptune's discovery marked the "arrival of the first wave of great Hindu and Buddhist teachers in the West." [199] It is also associated with the emergence of mystical organizations such as the Theosophical Society. Although many of us may not be familiar with theosophy, this association "became one of the defining cultural movements of the late nineteenth century." [200] The Theosophists, exemplified in the "remarkable charismatic Russian émigré" Helena Petrovna Blavatsky

(1931-1991), advocated that the best way to "take the entire world into its next great historical phase, a time of promised enlightenment, equality, peace and justice" was through "personal spiritual enlightenment." [201] Seen through another prism, these and related events presage the fact that over-reliance on religious viewpoints has led to serious social upheaval.

True to its archetypal reputation, the time of Neptune's discovery is not entirely clear. David McCann uses a 24 September 1846 date, with the time at 23:21 GMT (Berlin), which results in a Leo Rising (1°48"). Gary Caton notes the difficulty of pinpointing the time due to the "vague, second hand accounts of the time of discovery," plus the fact that all potential times of discovery occur during a period where the Ascendant is changing signs. [202] Caton concludes that the Cancer Rising chart (23:06:36 GMT) "says more about the intrinsic nature of Neptune as an archetype," while a Leo Rising chart "seems to better describe the later drama that unfolded between the British and the French over who to give credit for the discovery." [203] Both McCann and Caton note Neptune's close conjunction with Saturn in the sign (both at 25° Aquarius) and terms of Saturn. McCann comments, "it takes a lot of Saturn to bring Neptune down to earth," and adds that the conjunction is characteristic of the Victorian age: "hard working and capable, but often unable to find the balance between the materialistic and the visionary." [204] I would also highlight that Mars in Virgo in the 3rd house lies quincunx to Neptune in Aquarius in the 8th. This relationship connotes a similar energy—it takes a strong Mars in Virgo to get Neptune in Aquarius out of the clouds and into the world of reality. Caton takes a somewhat different track. Using a classical analysis, he notes that Saturn lies in a diurnal sign in a night chart, and as such is "the most potentially troublesome planet in the chart." The Neptune-Saturn conjunction tilts toward the negative manifestations of Saturn, such as tyranny and the upcoming era of social problems brought about by Industrialization. He also describes an "occluded" or opaque quality to 8th house matters (collective values and property, money, health) suggested by Neptune's placement "in aversion" to, or in the 8th whole sign house from, the Ascendant. Overall, Caton concludes that the Neptune-Saturn conjunction speaks to an "opening of boundaries" which has "potentially troublesome ramifications." [205]

A very active yod is also prominent in Neptune's discovery chart—not only is there the Mars-Neptune quincunx, but Mars also lies in quincunx to Pluto, with Pluto placed in sextile to Neptune-Saturn. These quincunxes call for some rather challenging adjustments, although the Mars in Virgo apex point suggests a platform of strength and focus supporting creative action. McCann correlates the Saturn-Mars-Pluto yod with the emergence of religious ideas, including the Taiping Rebellion (1850's) in China that sought the replacement of Confucianism and other

Eastern religions with Christianity. He also points to the Mormons' traveling to Utah (1856) to create their "theocratic community, and in 1848, "the Fox sisters produced the poltergeist manifestations that led to the spiritualist movement; even if they were frauds, that too is Neptunian." [206] Caton states that the yod represents further reinforcement of a malefic quality that is suggested by the Neptune-Saturn conjunction. As the Debility Lord of Cancer, Saturn takes away things of the 8th house. As such, it foreshadows the depletion of shared natural resources and the "tragic lack of limits on consumption." [207]

Some Implications –The Universe Widens Its Aperture and Reveals Other Astrological Dimensions

To recap, the flaws in the naming processes of Uranus and Neptune have prodded us to take a second look at the propriety of attaching Uranian and Neptunian meanings to the planets that ultimately came to be known as Uranus and Neptune. As a result of this undertaking, we have discovered the possibility that the astrological significance of Uranus and Neptune stems from events and movements that signaled worldwide social, economic and political changes. It is not simply that these events correlate to astrological keywords, but they in fact confer astrological significance. There is an important dynamic at play here, and it harkens back to ancient conceptions of universe-al unity. Contrary to the contemporary paradigm that rejects the non-observable and non-material, the implications of the process by which these planets have been authenticated draws us to a renewed appreciation of *"As Above, So Below"* connectivity and the operation of an ineffable unity that pervades physical manifestation. At the very least, it is as if the universe is using its own method of communication in order to underscore its desire to have us broaden and re-vision contemporary, ego-driven cosmology.

Astrologer and Hellenistic historian Chris Brennan provides further evidence that the universe—or at least Uranus and Neptune—may be encouraging astrologers in particular to attend these messages. His research indicates that over time, conjunctions between Uranus and Neptune are usually characterized by the following:

1. "A transmission of older astrological texts, often involving translations.
2. A sudden revival of older forms of astrology.
3. A synthesis of these older forms of astrology with whatever the prevailing contemporary astrological tradition is at the time." [208]

Of course, neither Neptune nor Uranus had been officially identified during much of this time frame and Brennan is not ascribing astrological significance on the basis of his research, but there is more than a hint of support for the intimate connection between these planets and events that augment astrological understanding. It does not seem so great a leap to move from noting this intimacy to a conclusion that these and similar events are so inextricably tied to these planets that they provide Neptune and Uranus with their respective *personae*.

There is another message which Uranus and Neptune impart. Over and above the substance of the events and movements that correlate to and support their names, these two post-Saturnian planets seem to be importuning us to "open your eyes and get ready for a new way, a new day." Unfortunately, many contemporary astrologers fail to appreciate the scope of this challenge, and essentially treat Uranus and Neptune as two more planets that occupy a flat, tropical zodiac. This is a mistake. As Gary Caton states when he analyzes the Uranus discovery chart, we may face decidedly "malefic and scorching consequences" unless we "patiently" increase our awareness about the new knowledge imparted by Uranus' appearance. [209] We may tend to "over-idealize the nature of this discovery" (Sun in Pisces as apex of Uranus opposing Mars / Saturn), but "we sorely need to engage our critical thinking skills with regard to it" (apex is in Virgo). [210] It may be that we will only appreciate Uranus' and Neptune's messages in hindsight, but it is as if the dam has broken. [211] Thus established, the momentum builds with the discovery of Pluto, then rolling onto dwarf planets, Kuiper Belt objects, Trans

Neptunian objects, and beyond. Uranus and Neptune signal there are not only new messages, but new types and categories of messages which point us to entirely different options and challenges.

5

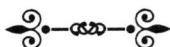

Pluto—The Copernican Paradigm Revisited

Pluto is commonly arrayed with Uranus and Neptune as an outer planet, although its discovery took place almost a century later (1930), well after Uranus, Neptune and many of the first asteroids. Although the process by which Pluto attained a name took place without the parochial strife that characterized Uranus' and Neptune's namings, there is a marked dissonance between Pluto's naming and his personality. Contrary to his reputation as the Dark Lord of the Underworld, Pluto obtained his designation with a process that can best be described as a "dreams-really-do-come-true" fairy tale. [212] Equally and perhaps more important as the circumstances of its naming, however, is the fact that today Pluto no longer retains planetary status: Pluto has been demoted from "planet" to "dwarf planet." While we may recognize that the astronomical community has modified its nomenclature regarding what constitutes a planet, we generally maintain that Pluto remains astrologically unchanged. There is considerable merit in this position, not the least of which is Pluto's history of demonstrable astrological significance. As we have seen with Uranus' and Neptune's namings, however, if we halt all inquiry into the foundation of Pluto's identity on the basis that "it works," we may overlook broader astrological messages. There is another problem, however, which astrologers have not addressed. It is the fact that we have failed to consider the astrology of the demotion itself. As will be discussed below, Pluto's demotion is such a "big deal" that it has led astronomers to revise their entire perception of the solar system. I suggest that when we employ an astrological lens to assess Pluto's reclassification, we may find an astrological paradigm shift as noteworthy as Copernicus' placement of the Sun, not the Earth, at the center of our solar system.

How Pluto Was Named

Pluto's naming presents an appealing and rather fortuitous story, although it was still a single individual who came up with the name. Its imprimatur also clearly arose from the astronomical community. Clyde Tombaugh at Lowell University is credited with the discovery in 1930. The photographs attesting to its presence were taken on January 23 and

29, but it was only on February 18th that Tombaugh realized he had discovered Pluto. [213] "In a pleasant gesture," the announcement of Pluto's discovery was delayed until the birthday of Percival Lowell, 13 March. [214] Prior to his death in 1916, Lowell was an American astronomer who had founded the Lowell Observatory in Flagstaff, Arizona, and for the last decade of his life had devoted a great deal of time searching for planet "X." [215] Following the announcement of the discovery, several names for the planetary body were proposed, including "Constance," which was the name of Mr. Lowell's wife. Mrs. Lowell also suggested "Zeus" and "Percival." The name "Pluto" eventually came from Venetia Burney, an 11-year-old schoolgirl from Oxford, England. [216] Ms. Burney had studied astronomy and mythology, and thought this planet's cold, dark presence quite nicely fit a god of the underworld.

Without denigrating the validity of her insight, a more detailed description of the story behind the naming of Pluto does not reflect quite as rosy a picture as we might imagine. Ms. Burney was not an astronomical outsider, or someone whose suggestion was chosen from a number of others because it was deemed most worthy. [217] Her uncle Henry Madan was a Science Master at Eton who in 1878 had suggested the names Phobos and Deimos for Mars' moons. Her interest in the planet was piqued by her grandfather Falconer Madan, a well-known figure who had retired from his post as librarian at the famous University of Oxford's Bodleian Library.[218] He was reading about the planet's discovery in *The London Times* and, after learning about it, Venetia was inspired to come up with a suitable name. Falconer was so impressed with his granddaughter's idea about naming the new planet Pluto that, while taking his daily constitutional, he dropped her suggestion in the mailbox of his acquaintance Herbert Hall Turner, professor of astronomy at Oxford. At that moment Turner was attending a meeting of the Royal Astronomical Society in London where there was much ado about what to name planet "X." Luckily, no one had thought of Pluto, and Professor Turner passed the suggestion along to his colleagues at the Lowell Observatory. The rest, as they say, "is history."

Although not directly involved with Pluto's naming, it is interesting that one of the glyphs for Pluto is comprised of the first two letters of Percival Lowell's name. Astrologers today seem to prefer the glyph for Pluto that follows the traditional pattern, which sets the Circle of Spirit within the Crescent of the Soul and above the Cross of Matter.[219] It is, however, difficult to miss the incongruity between the pleasantness of Burney's naming or the compassionate deference to Lowell, versus the ego focus of the initial glyph. Or, even more tellingly, the personable naming circumstances and Pluto himself—the ultimate annihilator, the "chilly lord of emptiness, the pitiless trickster [who] stares blankly and indifferently."[220] As its demotion eventually indicated, this double meaning may have presaged the fact that Pluto had more to say.

Correlations: Physical Features, Worldwide Events, Mundane Analysis

The July 2015 flyby of the New Horizons spacecraft has given us a great deal of new information about Pluto which reveal a number of correlations between its physical features and its astrological significations. [221] In fact, the correlations seem even more salient than those regarding Neptune and Uranus. One need only review the journey of the New Horizons project itself, beginning in 1989 with a group that called itself the "Pluto Underground," to discern a story of stark endings and regenerations that were transformed into a continuing series of surprises and awe. [222] It almost rivals the story of Neptune's discovery process! In looking to Pluto's physical features, the first and most descriptive word that arises is "ice." Whether made from nitrogen, methane or carbon dioxide, Pluto's dense, rocky core is held within an ice mantle, which may comprise up to 50% of its mass. [223] Ice intrinsically evokes Pluto's cold, implacable intensity and rigidity, as well a deep or instinctive truth that is shrouded, covert or hidden within. The New Horizons mission revealed a second feature of Pluto, which is an unexpected and "dazzling" complexity of landscapes. [224] It seems as if the more that is revealed about Pluto, the less we know about Pluto. This complexity reminds us of our astrological image of Pluto, where the surface belies a powerful, ever-changing reality. Pluto is not a mere homogeneous planet of gas, nor does it display the visually obvious diversity seen in Earth's oceans, land and people. Instead for example, Pluto shows us a "vast, craterless plain" that contains "icy, churning, convective cells 10 to 30 miles (16 to 48 kilometers) across." [225] This constantly regenerating plateau of ice lies within the stunningly heart-shaped but icy Tombaugh Region. The Wright Mons is a 2-mile high mountain of ice, which is 900 miles across and has a large hole in its center. Pluto has an unanticipated and hitherto unknown expanse of icy terrain that is described as "fretted," or "consisting of bright plains divided into polygon-shaped blocks by a network of dark, connected valleys typically reaching a few miles (3 to 4 kilometers) wide." [226] It is fascinating that one of Pluto's most distinguishing features lies with its icy heart, the Tombaugh Ridge. While no doubt an anthropomorphic characterization, it is difficult for us to view the Tombaugh "heart" and not perceive a visceral sense of the profound. This is not the heart of romance suggested by Venus, but rather a stark, determined message of actuality. Pluto's surface also reveals a geologically drawn, giant spider formation, consisting of at least six extensional fractures up to 360 miles long that converge to a center point, revealing red deposits below Pluto's surface. [227]

Interestingly, the brightness of Pluto's surface has changed between 1994 and 2003, which astronomers believe is due to the nature of its atmosphere, "extreme" axial tilt and orbital eccentricity. [228] This process evokes the potential for a formidable and multi-layered series of transformations—of the kind Pluto is known for. Pluto has at least 5 moons, including Charon, which was discovered in 1978. These moons have been named after underworld figures, although they follow the Pluto nomenclature rather than providing independent sources for Pluto's designation. [229] Interestingly, Charon is "tidally locked" with Pluto and always faces Pluto, so that it "neither rises nor sets, but hovers over the same spot on Pluto's surface." Charon is also so big that Pluto and Charon are sometimes referred to as a "double dwarf system." The intimacy of this connection is striking, suggesting Charon's wariness of a very powerful Pluto, or perhaps that Charon is "one of the gang." Not to be outdone, however, the Pluto-Charon orbit is the only known case of an orbit where its barycenter lies outside the physical body of either object, i.e. in outer space. Pluto's depths are indeed hard to pin down. [230]

Pluto's discovery in 1930 unmistakably correlates with significant global events. Foremost on any list of associations are worldwide war (1939-1945) and economic depression (stock market crash of 1929). These experiences were defined by violent upheavals, where power struggles seemed relentless, rulers were ruthless and the ends justified the means. Pluto's capacity to bring heretofore hidden or secret things to the surface is reflected in a number of other circumstances. On a microscopic level, on 7 March 1929, the Scottish chemist Alexander Fleming accidentally noticed that mold on a bacterial culture plate had created a bacteria free zone, which eventually became known as penicillin. [231] On a macroscopic level, Edwin Hubble announced on 17 January 1929 that galaxies were moving away from each other. [232]

Likely the most profound example of unearthing something that lies beneath the surface took place when scientists split the atom (1938), thus ushering in the Atomic Age. [233] The very word "subatomic" seems synonymous with Pluto and his realm of the Underworld. It triggered a heretofore unimaginable potential for utter annihilation and transformed our understanding about the frailty of the structure that lies beneath our everyday material world. On the other hand, truth and transformation do not always involve easy or pretty processes. Quantum physics was also born during this time period. Einstein published his famous conclusions regarding energy, matter and time in 1905 (special relativity) and 1916 (general relativity). Max Planck received the 1918 Nobel Prize in Physics for his work on quantum mechanics. [234] One of the most Plutonian of understandings generated by this new science is Werner Heisenberg's uncertainty principle, published in 1947. [235] Scientist and author David Cassidy states that the articulation of this principle represents a "profound and controversial *transformation* in our understanding of nature." (Italics added) The uncertainty or "indeterminacy" principle states that simultaneous measurement of two variables such as the position and momentum of a moving particle "entails a necessary limitation on precision." The more precise one measures a given variable, the more imprecise is the measurement of the other. As acknowledged by Robert Hand,

> "When you get to very small magnitudes (subatomic particles) and very large ones (the universe as a whole), or even when you consider some aspects of human behavior ("psychic" phenomena), objectivist science begins to lose its power to describe and predict, and studies start resembling metaphysics more than science." [236]

It is also not surprising that Pluto challenged previously held notions about human nature. Its discovery correlated with the development of psychology, as well as the stark reality of existentialism. [237] For example, astrologer, archetypal cosmologist, historian and author Richard Tarnas dates Carl Jung's (1875-1961) use of the term "synchronicity" to 1928. [238] In 1912 Marcel Duchamp completed "Nude Descending a Staircase, No. 2," a painting that attempts to depict the movement of descending with a series of interlocking planes. It had significant impact on modern and abstract art. [239] For astrologers, it is particularly fascinating to note the association between the discovery of Pluto on 18 February 1930 and the appearance in the British newspaper *Sunday Express* of the infant Princess Margaret's birth chart on 24 August 1930. As Nicholas Campion writes, "At the time, the <u>Express</u>'s move was an act of journalistic genius, a small but significant event, the consequences of which were to see astrology's triumphant re-entry to the public sphere." [240]

Pluto is situated in the 12th house in the chart of its discovery. [241] The 12th house has traditionally been described as a "temple of ill-omen, misery, bane and toil; hostile to future activity ... danger, infirmity, death ... enemies, imprisonment." [242] These descriptions strongly correlate with worldwide war, economic depression and the onset of the Atomic Age. Its placement in Cancer also emphasizes the negative impact these circumstances had on humanity's sense of physical and emotional security. As also observed by Gary Caton, Leo rises in the Pluto discovery chart, which nominates the Sun as its Chart Ruler or Domicile Lord. [243] The Sun's powerful status might initially appear to mitigate the bad tidings of the 12th house, but it is weakened by its placement in Aquarius (fall). The fact that the Sun is also at 29°49" of Aquarius evokes a similar uneven, or good-news-bad-news quality. As Caton observes, on the one hand, its advanced position within the sign suggests the completion of a long— and in this case very difficult process of upheaval; while on the other hand, when the Sun changes signs by progression, it enters the 8th house. If viewed as a horary chart, this movement from the "bright side "

(Sun in angular 7th house) to the "darker side" (8th as House of Death) foreshadows a "fundamental shift in context that will (eventually) render the original question moot and/or signal a major change in identity." [244] This sounds intriguingly close to Pluto's eventual re-classification. Pluto's downgrade is also presaged by its presence in the constellation Gemini, which highlights its dual nature. It is closer to Pollux than Castor, reflecting that it is "decidedly on the side of the dark twin Pollux." [245] Bernadette Brady describes Pollux as "crafty, spirited, rash, and connected to poisons," while Castor is "linked to keen intellectual and success in law and publishing [although] ... prone to violence." [246] Caton also points out that Mercury is near maximum elongation from the Sun, and due to retrograde motion, is in the zone of the sky that it crosses three times. Not only do these positions evoke the fact that Clyde Tombaugh had actually twice photographed Pluto's position before he reached his "Eureka moment" in identifying it a month later, but they also emphasize the evanescence of Pluto's identity and his proclivity to induce profound change. [247]

Venus in Pisces (exalt) is also conjunct the Royal star Formalhaut which has traditionally been seen as giving "a desire to pursue ideals, and even promises success with those ideals, but only if they are pursued for the collective good." [248] As we know, capitalism promised great economic opportunities and socialism / communism held the banner of social equality high, but these movements were ultimately perverted by those who sought political supremacy. This message is reiterated in a T-square where Venus is in Pisces (exalt), 8th house opposes Neptune in Virgo, 2nd house, and both square Jupiter in Gemini (Joy), 11th house. Caton sees the opposition as "too much of a good thing" and the "collective greed" that hides beneath Neptune's "mask." It is also reminiscent of the scientific discoveries that correlate to Pluto's discovery—much knowledge was unearthed, including the far-reaching recognition that our observations of reality may be "uncertain," but this awareness has also unfortunately been used to advance personal and geo-political interests. The Pluto discovery chart also displays an applying T-square formed by Saturn in Capricorn, 6th house opposing Pluto, both squaring Uranus in Aries, 9th house. If the former T-square speaks of beneficence to the point of destruction, this cadent T-Square suggests the opposite. Saturn, the boundary maker, is the Debility Lord of the Ascendant but is dignified as a result of its presence in Capricorn. Caton states that in such a case, Saturn's strength will likely be applied in a negative fashion. Unluckily for Saturn, it is also widely conjunct by latitude "one of the most malefic stars in the sky, Facies." A feisty Uranus, bristling with revolutionary zeal, hardly brings a calming force to the opposition between Saturn versus a poorly placed Pluto. I suggest that the boundary that is ultimately doomed to fall is that of our perception of the solar system. Pluto's challenges are nothing if not profound.

The Demotion of Pluto:
A Celestial Paradigm Change

The reclassification of Pluto as a minor planet in 2006 re-wrote the astronomical textbook's definitions of what constitutes a planet. It re-configured the celestial map and catalyzed a paradigm shift of the highest order, much as Copernicus did with his depiction of a heliocentric rather than a geocentric solar system. [249] Pluto's reclassification has much to teach us, and evokes the traditional image of Pluto as Plouton, the giver of riches and treasure. As recognized by depth psychologist James Hillman, "pictures of Pluto show his cornucopia like great ear, spilling over with fruitful possibilities of understanding." [250] I contend that we astrologers may not be fully aware of the full breadth of Pluto's treasure trove. Without delving too deeply, there is one simple reason that Pluto's reclassification should cause us to sit up and take notice, which is that at least in the visual sense, the resulting celestial reconfigurations underscore rather than take away from an astrological point of view. Before Pluto became a dwarf planet, most people thought our solar system contained less than a dozen, huge planetary spheres. With this mental image, it was easy for those seeking to disparage astrology to believe that it was impossible for these entities to resonate with, much less "influence" people or events. [251] Enter Pluto's demotion. Post-Pluto reveals a different vista, one packed with an uncountable number of extra-terrestrial bodies that display a myriad of sizes and shapes. These new bodies also interact with each other in new and interesting ways. They in fact interact in so many ways that astronomical nomenclature has been significantly re-drawn. Instead of a few, very large planetary billiard balls rolling around the solar system's pool table, the new solar system is filled with an uncountable number of players that are grouped into interlocking webs or tapestries of celestial teams. Although somewhat paradoxically but also importantly for astrology, this re-vision situates planetary bodies within a more proportionate frame of reference. It is not just big planets "out there" and we humans "here," but lots of celestial entities that comprise the "we" of our solar system. Perhaps most importantly, this disorganized unity—or unified disorganization—not only implies "we are all in this together," but that there is a larger, underlying framework of co-creation animating the entire process. Indeed, it may be that as we humans are learning more about the cosmos, the cosmos is learning more about itself. We are each acting as partners in an ongoing process of creation, or *"As Around, So Within."* The egg that Copernicus and his scientific progeny broke is moving back to alignment, and it is up to us to use an astrological vocabulary to tell us what that signifies.

Astronomers have explicitly recognized the paradigmatic nature of the changes elicited as a result of Pluto's redefinition. Dr. Alan Stern, who has been previously mentioned herein as an astrophysicist and principal investigator for the New Horizons mission to Pluto, characterizes this reclassification as instituting a "revolution in the geography of the solar system." [252] Using his analysis, our solar system has for quite some time been seen as being comprised of 4 terrestrial planets (including Earth) and 4 gas giants, plus the later addition of one "misfit"—Pluto. This view of the solar system held sway until the 1990's when it was discovered that Pluto was not in fact a lone misfit, but was "just the brightest and first discovered of a very large number of planetary bodies" in the most distant region of our solar system. Stern states that instead of two planetary clumps, plus one planet, astronomers now think and talk about three *belts* or *zones* of celestial bodies that come in all shapes and sizes. [253] The previous mental image of the solar system based on discrete, clearly identifiable and big entities, has shifted to one populated by bands of non-uniform objects that are difficult to observe—even with the latest in astronomical technology. As a result of these discoveries, an entirely different system of nomenclature was required—hence, the demotion of Pluto to "dwarf planet" status. Intriguingly, Stern also notes that Pluto exhibits "very exotic physics" that stem from its small size, coupled with a disproportionately large atmosphere. [254] Astronomical observations reflect that this atmosphere is also melting away from Pluto in a hydrodynamic "escape process" which, when measured in geologic time, is taking place at a rapid rate. A similar "escape process" is believed to have helped shape ancient Earth's atmosphere. No other planetary body in our solar system currently exhibits this process, and scientists hypothesize that Pluto's evolution may uncover important information about Earth's evolution as well. Although there are competing theories, most scientists also believe that another planet smashed into Pluto, forming satellites, much in the same manner as our Moon was shaped as a result of a collision between the Earth and a Mars-sized body. [255] Pluto's hidden treasures continue to be mined, as befits the Lord of the Underworld.

Before further evaluating Pluto's reclassification, it is only fair to acknowledge that the planetary entity that bumped Pluto from its pedestal was Eris. In so doing, the goddess of discord seems to have accomplished her task with consummate brio! The planet Eris was discovered by Michael Brown in 2005 and at the time appeared to be larger than Pluto. [256] NASA initially described it as the solar system's tenth planet, but when it became clear that other similarly sized planetary objects were likely to be discovered, the IAU redefined or "demoted" Pluto. [257] Since then, Eris has been shown to be slightly smaller than Pluto. For purposes of our discussion here, although Eris undoubtedly had her hand in Pluto's reformulation, there had to be something in place first, before a change could come about. That "something" was Pluto's reclassification. Importantly, it is the *demotion* of Pluto and not the planetary body itself that transformed our understanding about the cosmos. Our conception of Pluto and the solar system was significantly revised, but the planetary body named Pluto remains unchanged. Another way of phrasing it might be that while Pluto may have been the pedestal "bumpee" rather than the "bumper [Eris]," it was the "bumping [the demotion]" that occasioned the fundamental change. Because "Pluto's demotion" does not roll off the tongue quite as easily, I have adopted the phrase "Post-Pluto" to refer to the reclassification and its *sequelae*. There is also an intriguing quality of undercover power or sabotage that gives extra punch to Pluto's claim to fame here—as if Pluto knew all along that we were being hoodwinked and he covertly bided his time until we had to acknowledge reality. There is also no reason to anticipate that current models of our solar (much less galactic) system will remain as currently conceived. Rankings based upon astronomical characteristics, such as diameter and mass, demonstrate that Pluto has been forced to cede ground to a number of other planetary entities, and there are legions of others yet to be discovered that will likely push Pluto even further down similar lists. True to his astrological significance, Post-Pluto not only represents transformation, but a *continual process of transforming*. In sum, it may very well come to pass that Pluto and Eris will be seen as co-conspirators, but I submit that the reverberations from Pluto's demotion give it a distinct edge in the Copernican awards contest.

As might be expected, Pluto's demotion fueled public uproar. One might also have anticipated this demotion to trigger a commensurate firestorm of re-evaluation within the astrological community, but the fires of controversy were more tamped down than ramped up. It is as if we astrologers were being presented with an eclipse of Pluto, but we devoted less attention to it than analogous lunar events. Despite the historic nature of the downgrade, one would be hard pressed to find an astrologer who modified the astrological significance of Pluto in her or his work. Notably, not much print space has been devoted to the demotion either. A welcome exception to this stance can be found in Robert Hand's presentation in 2014 regarding the Uranus—Pluto cycle. [258] Hand was not timid about asking the question: should astrologers continue to treat Pluto as equal to the other planets? His response to the question was "yes," largely because Pluto was "still manifesting." [259] He also cited the fact that from 578 BCE to 2385 CE, all seven of the Neptune-Pluto conjunctions occur within a small 10° area, and no other pairs of bodies in our solar system act in this manner. Hand characterized this astronomical configuration as a set of mutual planetary (not satellite-to-planet) aspects or resonances where each cycle is inherent to both planets. While this is an intriguing concept, I am not convinced that the door is shut on our inquiry. One might ask if Neptune should thereby be reclassified, or the unit of resonance as opposed to the separate planetary entities themselves constellates astrological significance. It is also unclear that, given the pace of astronomical discoveries, whether this anomaly will be one-of-a-kind.

More important than astrologers' tepid reaction to Pluto's reclassification, however, is the fact that while we have acknowledged *the fact* of the reclassification, we have yet to analyze the *underlying meaning* of the demotion. We continued this avoidant posture even as more and more celestial bodies became identified. Instead of examining these circumstances, we simply lowered the bar of astrological significance. Unfortunately, however generous our motives may have been, we have implicitly sanctioned a kitchen-sink method for ascribing astrological significance. Just because an entity is "out there" or we have a pre-existing schema that worked for pre-Plutonian planets does not necessarily substantiate its inclusion in today's charts. A central tenet here is that we should examine whether and how to respond to Pluto's reclassification without automatically conferring astrological significance upon all celestial bodies. Salient questions include - how do we ascribe significance in this environment? Do all celestial bodies have astrological significance, and in the same degree? What new factors or types of factors can or should be used to assess astrological significance? What kind of relationship between astronomy and astrology should there be? Even more importantly and as newer celestial bodies are identified, what does it mean that we are dealing with a process of transforming, and not just a discrete change from celestial platform A to celestial platform B?

The thorniness of these questions uncovers a wealth of opportunities for the evolution of astrological analysis and knowledge. And pursuing them underscores Plato's reputation for pushing us to acknowledge ultimate truths, whether we like the idea of "ultimate truth" or not. When thinking about the impact of Pluto's demotion in this context, I am reminded of Shakespeare's observation, "Now let it work. Mischief thou art afoot. Take thou what course thou wilt." [260]

Mundane Analysis Regarding Pluto's Reclassification

Pluto's reclassification chart confirms the paradigmatic scope of the challenges it has catalyzed. The official announcement of Pluto's demotion took place at the close of the 26th General Assembly for the International Astronomical Union, on 24 August 2006 at 6 p.m. CEDT in Prague, Czech Republic. [261] A preliminary overview of the Pluto reclassification chart reveals a striking series of oppositions. On one side of the chart we find Neptune lying in the 2nd house, Aquarius and Uranus in the 3rd house, Pisces. [262] Opposing Neptune are Mercury, Saturn and Venus in the 8th House, Leo, and opposing Uranus are the Sun, Moon and Mars in the 9th House, Virgo. [263]

This arrangement places the personal planets (Mars, Moon, Sun, Mercury, Venus) in the Third Quadrant that is inter-personal, looks outward and seeks to connect with others, while both Neptune and Uranus reside in the First Quadrant that connotes internal personhood and unique value. These oppositions expose the fundamental question that lies at the heart of how we will or will not adapt to the classification: do we continue to hold onto an identity based upon familiar but eroding solar system maps or are we willing to delve into other perspectives, which will likely take us into unknown but transformative territories? Not an easy task, but one that will be difficult to avoid. It is also important to recognize the special relevance to astrologers of Neptune's opposition to a combust Mercury in the 9th house.[264] The 9th House of the Sun historically connoted "probing the grander mysteries," and was linked to revelations, prophecy and soothsaying. [265] Although we may be more comfortable with associating ourselves with the "grander mysteries" than divination, Mercury's placement highlights an astrological signature. [266] Neptune also in Mercury's house—the 3rd, which is the house of peer-to-peer exchanges. As if that weren't sufficient, Neptune and Uranus, as well as the Sun and Mercury, lie in mutual reception. As we can see from these placements, Neptune and Uranus appear to know each other well and will likely cooperate with each other in order to achieve mutual aims. They did so by arriving when they did—accompanied by worldwide events that point to the need for us to be mindful of the Earth and its occupants. It is of particular salience that this partnership lies in the Pluto reclassification chart, connoting that our awareness of Uranus and Neptune constituted a first step towards a more encompassing truth about the cosmos. The universe seems to be sending a particularly strong message to astrologers, perhaps because we are uniquely situated to hear it.

These multi-planet oppositions are not the only evidence that Pluto's reclassification presents a dilemma of difficult but necessary choices. We need go no further than the fact that the non-personal and "outer" planets Neptune and Uranus lie in unfamiliar territory, i.e. the First Quadrant that signals inwardly-defined individuality. Neptune also provides a fluid uncertainty to this identity, and Uranus injects an unpredictable changeability into the mix. [267] Gary Caton amplifies these observations by pointing out that all the trans-personal planets are in trans-personal signs (Aquarius, Pisces, Pluto in Sagittarius). [268] He concludes that this "'trans-personal crescendo'" represents a "collective wake-up call to get real about what we've done to Earth since the discovery of the modern planets." In order to reach for these goals, it likely requires an awakening that needs to take place on an individual basis.

Two T-square like aspects in the Pluto reclassification chart provide additional confirmation to these themes. The configurations include: (1) Jupiter in the 10th house, Scorpio as the focal point for the 2nd house Neptune opposition to the 8th house containing Mercury, Saturn and Venus, and (2) allowing for some generosity in orbs, Pluto in in the 12th house, Sagittarius occupying a similar position with respect to the 3rd House Uranus opposition to the Sun, Moon and Mars in the 9th. While Pluto and Jupiter do not directly aspect each other, they lie in signs of mutual reception. This, plus their 11th and 12th house placements, connotes a powerful and deeply profound re-visioning. This quality is strengthened by the mutual receptions between Neptune and Uranus, and Mercury and the Sun. There seems to be a lot of cooperation here—on planetary as well as human levels. As earlier discussed, these aspect patterns suggest that grappling with Pluto's new status will require our participation as a community of peers and involve deep soul-searching on a group, as well as on an individual basis. Something is going to end here (Pluto in 12th), and this something will likely be our personal beliefs (Sagittarius) about the solar system. Lest we have any doubt about the level of Pluto's transformative energy here, it lies conjunct the Galactic Center. Even Eris lies trine to Pluto, suggesting an alliance, albeit a fiery one (Eris in Aries, 4th house), rather than outright warfare. [269] As more fully discussed below, the so-called downgrading of Pluto paradoxically presages profound creative potential. It is up to astrologers to figure it out (Gemini opposite Sagittarius) and bring it down to earth (Taurus opposite Scorpio).

As earlier mentioned, it is truly amazing that only 400 of the 10,000 International Astronomical Union members were present and affirmatively voted for the adoption of the resolution effecting this ground-breaking (read as: solar system-breaking) change. Gary Caton's analysis of IAU's actions regarding Pluto underscores the point that abject reliance upon the IAU decree is not the answer. With Capricorn rising, the reclassification chart has the "classic signature of an 'inside job'" and "hidden power plays" (Midheaven in Scorpio). The star Vega is also conjunct with the Ascendant, thereby reflecting that the "announcement is at least as much performance as it is science." Lest we attempt a quick fix of IAU's declaration by closing our eyes to Pluto's reclassification, Caton notes that the fall Lord of Capricorn is Jupiter. Jupiter lies in the 11ᵗʰ house (Joy), as does the Midheaven. As a result of these placements, Caton concludes that the IAU's "achievement" has "some staying power," and that the "door has been seemingly permanently shut on a first world of eight proper planets." It is not likely that Pluto will ever return to "regular" planetary status. And denial is not an option.

Further Suggestions about the Meaning of Pluto's Reclassification

The Post-Pluto paradigm not only suggests intriguing questions about the nature of astrological significance, but has broad implications for a new, or renewed, appreciation of the cosmos. We have seen that the naming processes surrounding Uranus, Neptune and Pluto sought to direct us from personal and inter-personal perspectives to worldwide problems and concerns. [270] Pluto's change in status offers an even more expansive vista. The following outlines some thoughts about them.

Pluto's do-over has flung a gauntlet at humanity's efforts to impose limits. Throughout history we have alternately latched onto Saturn as the ultimate solar system limit, then Neptune, and then Pluto. These limits, however, have been found to be not as limiting as we once thought. Once Pluto lost its "outer limit" status and ushered in an era of exoplanets and 11,000-year solar orbits, it exposed the futility of humanity's continuing efforts to delimit space. Pluto is saying something not just about celestial space, but the generic futility of limit-making. Humans instinctively gravitate towards circumscribing things, thereby keeping family close and fencing danger out. Limits are comforting, and they provide a sense of regularity, security, that "all is well." The roots of this tendency may be tribal and territorial, but they continue to have a significant impact on how we operate within our environment. Limits also carry important drawbacks. For example, they are implicitly predicated upon black-and-white configurations. One is either in, or out; this one is good, but that one is bad. They presume linearity and hierarchy. I am up, and you are down; we are better and you are worse. An important limit that Pluto may be aiming his sights upon is zealotry—we are the true believers and you are wicked apostates; we have the truth on our side, and—well, you know the rest.

Pluto's message that we may never enjoy the embrace of an ultimate celestial limit also contains the seeds for human affirmation. Instead of investing energy in drawing go / no borders, we can learn to embrace each other. If help is not "out there," an opportunity opens for us to look more fully within and among ourselves for sustenance. Instead of navigating existence with a me-versus-you or us-versus-them paradigm, or looking for a white knight or savior to redeem us, we can shift our focus to me-*and*-you, and inter-connection rather than conflict. We may need to come up with a better and more inclusive way of human interaction—one that celebrates differences but also brings us together.

We can also observe that change, rather than stasis or *status quo*, is the new norm. One never knows if a new planet might swing into astronomical view, tracing a small section of its multi-century solar orbit. The changes wrought by Pluto's demotion are likely not the last to come. We now perceive the dynamic quality of the universe, where planets smash into each other, coalesce into planetary entities and capture celestial bodies. One change presages another, and one day we may need to consider whether and how to incorporate non-solar system bodies into our charts. What about nearby galaxies, or dark matter?

What might the impact be of the cosmic glue suggested by Higgs-Boson theoreticians—does it trace a path to discovering, at least in part, why astrology "works?"

A corollary to Pluto's message of limitlessness is his assault on the concept of classification and categorizing. As discussed above when introducing the subject of the proliferation of planetary and celestial bodies, "dwarf planet" retains its place in today's astronomical nomenclature. It is, however, unclear whether this designation can withstand continued scientific and astronomical scrutiny. Not only do the current IAU definitions fail to accurately describe the celestial entities we now know about, but it is unlikely that they will continue to fit the astronomical definitional structure of the future. [271] The heart of the matter, however, is not that categories are wrong or require revision as new data is received, but that classifications themselves are inherently arbitrary and entirely relative to those forming them. While providing information, they do not supply the "final" answer or even the whole picture. Post-Pluto leads us beyond categorical reality to one that is dimensional or multi-dimensional.

Another sticky issue Post-Pluto raises is that, if ever there were a doubt, our place in the universe is not the exalted one we might have once perceived or preferred. We may therefore need to exert greater efforts in getting our own planet in order. It may be that if we did not get the messages suggested by Uranus and Neptune about tending to the health of our home planet Earth, Pluto has added a mighty voice of his own.

Post-Pluto: "As Around, So Within"

The change in Pluto's planetary status threw a monkey wrench into the modern model of the solar system, but it also signaled that it is time to reassess and renew extant astrological perspectives. As described by Alan Stern above, astronomers took up this challenge by "revolutionizing" the geography of the solar system. Although they struggled, and still struggle, with the classification of new celestial bodies, they also avoided falling down the "rabbit hole" of inserting celestial bodies into their familiar model. Pluto's reassignment opens a similar space for astrologers, although the challenge is more complicated than simple cartographical rearrangement. Undoubtedly not its last or final iteration, the cosmic aperture seems to have widened, signaling the potentiation of a more deeply textured *astro-logos*. While "*As Above, So Below*" continues to be an axiom we rely upon, another dimension of this truth has emerged: "*As Around, So Within.*"

In place of a solar system composed of a few prominent parts, we are now presented with a whole that is made up of so many parts that singling out seven, eight, eleven or some other number for sole attention seems misguided. [272] The new parts also differ from previously classified bodies, as well as among themselves—in size, mass and density, shape, distance from Earth and/or each other, and so on. Just as, importantly, they interact. These circumstances beg us to look above, behind and/or around the new celestial bodies and discern *if* there is a larger pattern. And *what* that pattern might be. The emergence of the newfound celestial array may also be asking us to dig deeply within ourselves, to resist the urge to apply our current interpretative frameworks and to allow ourselves to formulate alternative understandings. At the least, more fractiousness suggests greater possibilities for shared commonality. There are more opportunities to recognize common ground within a diverse group or series of groups than if we number one, seven or twelve. Importantly, not only do the new celestial bodies display different physical and astronomically defined characteristics, but their *en masse* appearance—or, more to the point, our apprehension of their presence—suggests an entirely different process or state of being. We can no longer limit our vision to the one or two-dimensional frame of up-there and down-here. Instead, we need to look within and around ourselves and utilize multidimensional perspectives.

Our belief that solar system was comprised of 8 planets (including Earth) existed for millennia. As Uranus (1781), Neptune (1846) and Pluto (1930) came to light, the seeds for a new framework were already being sown. As discussed above, while not entirely jettisoning the classical, Earth observation-based method for ascribing astrological significance, these planets' identities are most clearly established by their correlations to worldwide phenomena. This new methodology suggests that our astrological and cosmological depth of field was being widened, albeit at a measured tempo. This tempo quickened and on one single day, 24 August 2006, Pluto was demoted to dwarf planet status. As a result of this reconfiguration, the solar system as we knew it was no more. It is as if the Uranus-to-Pluto [273] time frame signaled the opening bell and first few laps of a new, fundamentally different cosmological relay race, but the pace picked up considerably and, with Pluto's reclassification, took off at warp speed. This relay race opens with the basics of essential race preparation and training that are demonstrated by the development of classical planetary identities, the next phase is the beginning of the race—here are the discoveries of the modern planets and their correlation with Earth-wide events, and the conclusion of the race (or the first heat in the race) is the Post-Pluto sprint. The first theme of this analogy is, of course, that this race could not have been run without each of the constituent elements. There is also a gradual, step-by-step awakening to planetary realities, including the reality that we humans must tend to the impact we are having on our world, or face the consequences. We exist not only as individuals, tribe members or citizens of larger political entities, but the discoveries of Uranus,

Neptune and Pluto remind us that we also occupy a planet called Earth. Post-Pluto takes us even farther and spotlights our membership in the solar system.

In a message that seems particularly relevant to astrologers, Post-Pluto also reprises and revises astrology's oft-quoted principle *"As Above, So Below."* As earlier discussed when considering the ancient paradigm that supports classical planets' astrological legitimacy, the *"As Above"* planets resonate, influence, correspond or have consonance with *"So Below"* human beings. This model sounds a great deal like the classical model of the solar system—one that is populated with a few planets that interact within a more or less contained system. Discovery of the modern planets added more denizens to our solar system, but we were still in integer territory. There is also a third and arguably the most fundamental part of the *"As Above, So Below"* mantra that posits a whole, a unity or an underlying principle that connects and co-creates the *"Above"* and *"Below."* This leg of the model is unfortunately not often included in contemporary astrological explications. Our apparent collective amnesia about this most important aspect of the original maxim may be that it sounds theistic or deistic, and in accordance with scientific proclivities, it is easier to identify and catalogue items in box A and box B than talk about wholes or unities. At its heart, Post-Pluto is not exhorting us to worship a deity, but at minimum it is suggesting that the *"Below"* and *"Above"* sides of the astrological coin need to be recognized

and re-connected. Because we now realize that celestial entities number into infinity and we now have
a solar system that is organized into belts, or groups
of such entities, Post-Pluto adds more to "As Above,
So Below," and guides us to an understanding of "*As
Around, So Within*."

There is a final nuance to Post-Pluto that may
be the most important, particularly for astrologers. It
is not only that "*Above*" should be re-connected with
"*Below*," but that there is an order or pattern that is
distinct from that which is "up" and that which is
"down here." There are too many dynamic, interacting celestial entities "*Around*" us in order to perceive
our universe through "up" and "down" glasses, and
using the race relay metaphor, the Post-Pluto reality denotes more than the sum of its parts. Needless
to say, we are not dealing with the scientific paradigm that explains the universe predicated upon the
operation of mechanical forces and an emphasis on
reason, progress and individualism. [274] Although undoubtedly instructive, Post-Pluto also cannot be re-
duced to the discoveries of quantum physics. [275] Instead of absolute uncertainty, we are dealing with a
direction, the formulation of an intent or a design.
The essential point here is that the serial accretion
of new information about our solar system suggests
the unfolding of an underlying order or pattern, the
"*Within*." We did not learn about Ceres or Sedna before we knew about Uranus and Neptune, or even
Mars and the Moon. The "*As Around, So Within*"

paradigm also suggests that the cosmos is learning about itself a as we are learning about the cosmos. Each informs and animates the other, and all partake of a greater and ongoing process of co-creation. As Robert Hand suggests, the "universe [i]s a living entity . . . where psyche and cosmos are one." [276] And, "the physical plane . . . [is] the place where God is in a state of becoming rather than being. And what we are all doing here is doing that becoming." [277] To be clear, Post-Pluto also does not suggest that we are returning to the Platonic-Pythagorean view of *kosmos,* as described by Richard Tarnas, as "*intelligent* order, *beauty,* and structural *perfection*" (emphases added). [278] Nicholas Campion adds,

> "[Plato] believed that the material, phenomenal world inhabited by humanity may be seen as an illusion resting in a real world consisting of 'soul,' conceived as thoughtful, intelligent, benevolent reason and emanating from the mind of a creator, a remote, impersonal God, best conceived of as a creative intelligence, the source of reason and good (itself defined as stability and order) and described by words such as father or maker and constructor of the universe. . . ." [279]

However appealing, Post-Pluto does not connote an ideal or perfection, or even pure intelligence or good that supersedes everyday reality. Not only would it be foolhardy to dismiss the genuine discoveries of science, but the Platonic view is static and perpetuates an inherent dualism (soul versus matter, for example). [280] Post-Pluto may be described as theater or a drama, but it is not a morality play. Neither humanity nor the cosmos has experienced the climax, nor even the dénouement of the play titled "*As Around, So Within*," but hopefully we can allow ourselves to plumb its Post-Plutonic riches.

At the least, Post-Pluto beckons us to take the step of observing the newfound marvels of our sky. In order to perceive what is ahead, we should complete the circle and embrace our ancient roots of celestial observation and the unity paradigm that inspired the development of astrology in the first place. Instead of remaining solely wedded to two-dimensional charts, we should take a good look at the celestial bowl, using our eyes, telescopes and computer imagery. As we have seen, our ancestors drew no sharp distinction between astrology and astronomy. As we have also seen, this ancient knowledge was neither "primitive," nor based upon magical speculation, but represented a highly sophisticated *zeitgeist*. Bernadette Brady points out, "[o]ur modern western mind has been moulded by reductionism: the pursuit of truth by the technique of breaking everything down to its simplest units in order to gain understanding." [281] Although this approach has brought significant material benefits to our modern world, it is not easily applied to the sky. Instead, Brady importunes us reach beyond the two-dimensional ecliptic and directly observe the sky itself, concluding,

> "I know that many astrologers prefer this method of working with fixed stars but I am deeply uncomfortable with it; for me it is like loving butterflies by sticking them onto blotting paper. I want my stars to be free, I want to rejoice at their rebirth, marvel at their resurrections and most importantly I want to honor their stories." [282]

Post-Pluto is *not* asking us to become ancient Babylonians. We should not avoid the truths imparted by contemporary experience, but neither should we stagnate within them.

6

Naming Of Newer Celestial Bodies—The Beat Goes On

The naming of celestial bodies without sufficient mooring in archetypal foundations did not end with Pluto's reclassification. On the contrary, the naming of newly-discovered bodies has accelerated to the point of routine normalcy. These newly detected bodies cannot remotely claim to have names that have "stood the test of time," and their naming processes continue to be characterized by haphazard, often parochial features. Once named, the "tail wagged the dog"—astrologers ratified these names and accorded them astrological significance. The naming processes surrounding Chiron and Haumea demonstrate these shortcomings.

Chiron

While inspired, Chiron's name was chosen because one man thought it was as good or better than any other choice he could make. On 18 October 1977, American astronomer Charles Kowal located Chiron in the Kuiper Belt near the edge of the solar system. It was near the orbit of Uranus, but on the other side of the sky. [283] Its orbit looked as if it was a comet, but it was at least 10 times larger than typical comets. Kowal comments,

> "When this discovery was reported to the news media, they immediately hailed it as a 'possible tenth planet.' It did not help matters any, because I didn't know what to call it! It is curious how people need to label things, and place everything in pigeonholes. Chiron simply does not fit in any pigeonhole. It remains unique, and giving it a label will not bring us any closer to an understanding of the true nature of this remarkable object." [284]

Kowal was also frustrated that the asteroid-naming process had become "trivialized." [285] One wonders how incensed Kowal might be today, as it appears that "cats, celebrities and fictional creatures all have a home" in the asteroid belt. [286] A sampling of these names include Monty Python—13681, Jab-

berwock—7470, Tomhanks - 12818 and Megry-
an—8353. In casting about for a name and desiring
to return to more familiar planetary designations,
Kowal found that the names of the centaurs had not
yet been used for any asteroids. Since Chiron was the
most famous of Centaurs, *presto*—Chiron. Kowal also
pointed out that Chiron's orbit, which comes close to
both Uranus and Saturn, fits with its mythological
roles as the son of Saturn and grandson of Uranus.
This rationale was not, however, why Chiron came
to be named as it did, although it fit nicely into the
more traditional scheme.

Attempting to establish associations between
Chiron and its physical features is difficult, given
its distance, but they are present. The International
Astronomical Union initially determined it was an
asteroid, but in 1988, astronomers observed an "apparent outburst in brightness," and in 1989, a trail-
ing coma was seen. [287] In 1991, the IAU officially
designated Chiron as a "captured comet." According
to the IAU, minor planets can be dwarf planets and
asteroids, but they are not supposed to be comets. [288]
Chiron is apparently an exception to that rule and is
also classified as a minor planet. NASA sources admit
that the true identity of centaurs continues to be "one
of the enduring mysteries of astrophysics." [289] Un-
certainties remain whether they are asteroids "flung
out" from the inner solar system or comets traveling toward the Sun "from afar." Recent information
from NASA's Wide-field Infrared Survey Explorer

("WISE") indicate their origin is cometary. Intriguingly, James Bauer, PhD, working at NASA's Jet Propulsion Laboratory in Pasadena, California notes, "[j]ust like the mythical creatures, the centaur objects seem to lead a double life" and come from deep space. Bauer is presumably referring to the mythological description of centaurs as having a human torso and head, with the body and legs of a horse. The reference to travel from deep space, however, strongly evokes the mythological and astrological image of Chiron as one who signals the potential for special or mystical knowledge—knowledge that fails to fit into ordinary Earth-bound parameters. This quality is also reflected in Chiron's eccentric orbit, which crosses the orbits of both Saturn and Uranus but also comes close to both planets. There is a near-is-far and far-is-near quality that permeates this movement. It also corresponds to Chiron's astrological role of a "mediator" between Saturn and Uranus, or "a link between the 'Guardian of the Spheres' (Saturn) and the outer planets." [290] Recognition of the associations between Chiron's physical features and the mythological centaur are intriguing and one might be tempted to return to classical planetary methods in justifying its astrological identity. On the other hand, it is unlikely that we have the full picture regarding its features.

According to astrologer Martin Lass, Chiron's "natal" chart (dated 1 November 1977) correlates to its astrological significance. [291] He primarily bases this conclusion on the close conjunction of Pluto and the North Node in Libra. Venus is also conjunct, with a 4°30' orb. Lass refers to Libra's position in the discovery chart as the "coming out" or "coming of age" point, where our focus on self "begins to give way to an acknowledgment of the Other in our lives." These Libran conjunctions reflect the "death of old illusions" and a "return to balance" that Chiron's call to healing and the evolution of spirit evoke. As discussed above, the date Chiron was discovered is actually 18 October 1977. A chart using this date also places Mercury and the Sun in Libra. There is clearly a significant focus on Libra. Importantly, Chiron is also retrograde and lies in Taurus that suggests Chiron is beckoning us to retreat to a place of silence—perhaps under a tree—and simply listen.

In a manner similar to that demonstrated regarding the non-classical planets, there is evidence that Chiron's designation is associated with global events. In the 1980s, astrologer and author Barbara Hand Clow stated that Chiron's appearance correlates with the rebirth in the 1970s of visionary breakthroughs, spontaneous channeling, divination, body/mind healing, homeopathic medicine, and "multi-dimensional perceptual skills." [292] Clow also interviewed a number of individuals who provided evidence for the correlation between the discovery of Chiron and the resurgence of spiritual healing following the "waves of blackness and fear which swept the Earth in the 1930's." One of these individuals was Matthew Fox who began his Creation Spirituality Movement in

Chicago on 5 November 1977. Jean Houston, Patricia Sun, PPMH Atwater, Jose Arguelles, Chris Griscom, Dr. Brugh Joy and David Spangler all reported that their "central teachings broke through" in the fall of 1977. [293] While I am not as familiar with these events, they do not seem to represent quite as impressive a swath of occurrences as those which took place surrounding the discoveries of Neptune, Uranus or Pluto. I therefore have some question that they support the naming of Chiron. Apparently, so do astrologers David Cochrane and astro-programmer John Halloran who have independently presented new findings about Chiron's essential meanings and significations, clearly demonstrating that Chiron is very much a work-in-progress over forty years after its discovery.

The exchange regarding Chiron began with John Halloran's piece on the "Nature of Chiron," in the International Society for Astrological Research (hereafter referred to as "ISAR"), Vol. 799, 21 July 2014. As a result of his research, Halloran stated that Chiron is not "just the asteroid of wounds and healing, [but] it is time to think about Chiron as the higher octave of Jupiter." Astrologer J. Lee Lehmann takes Halloran to task about attempting to "extract meaning from sources which themselves are completely undocumented . . . and are therefore less convincing." [294] David Cochrane's response to Halloran ("On Chiron Research," ISAR Vol 800) was to cite his own research which indicated that Chiron "gives one the ability to channel the spontaneity of Uranus in a well-defined structure." To this discussion I say, "bring it on." This is exactly the kind of debate astrologers should be having.

Regardless of whether one accepts the results of Clow's research, the fact remains that one individual astronomer bestowed astrological significance to a minor planet/cometary body that became known as Chiron. However strong the correlations between the physical features of Chiron and our astrological understanding of its significance, we must acknowledge that Chiron is not the same kind of planet as the Moon or Jupiter, or even Uranus and Neptune. Astrologers should at least consider whether and how it should be so designated. It may in fact be that Chiron's importance lies precisely in the fact that it is *not* a planet, and that it exhibits *dual* celestial qualities. A number of epistemological and spiritual implications flow from the nature of this manifestation. If it is bringing light from the far reaches of space, we owe it to Chiron to ponder its uniqueness.

Haumea

Haumea's naming process is considerably more complicated than Chiron's. Before Haumea's discovery and since about 1992, a number of celestial objects, such as Sedna (2003) and Quaoar (2002), had been identified. The spirit of astronomical discovery was in the air, which presaged the virtual deluge of "discoveries" yet to come. On 28 December 2004, while looking at some photographic plates generated in 2003, Michael Brown and two other CalTech astronomers, Chad Trujillo and David Rabinowitz, observed the celestial body that came to be known as Haumea. [295] As to naming Haumea, it "being only a few days after Christmas, [Brown] immediately nicknamed it 'Santa.'" Acknowledging the considerable tension between "doing careful work to make a complete announcement and doing an instant but incomplete announcement in order to make sure you don't get scooped," the Cal-Tech team choose to delay filing a report of these observations to the official IAU clearinghouse, the Minor Planet Center ("MPC") in Cambridge, Massachusetts. [296] By 7 July 2005, as he was "putting the finishing touches" on his paper regarding Haumea, his daughter Lilah was born, which further delayed the official announcement. He was about to do so, when to his "horror" Brown discovered that 39 hours before, two Spanish astronomers Pablo Santos-Sanz and Jose Luis Ortiz Moreno had filed papers with the IAU claiming their discovery of the same planetary body.

As can be imagined and because the mystery of what "really" happened will likely never be completely resolved, much controversy surrounds who should legitimately claim bragging rights as to Haumea's discovery. In support of their claim, the Spanish astronomers state that they had identified a planetary body, which was ultimately Haumea, while reviewing a two-year old backlog of celestial photos. They saw an object and were not sure whether it had been previously identified. On 26 July 2005, they came across the observation logs relating to Haumea posted by the Cal-Tech team, although the logs supposedly contained insufficient information to determine if they were looking at the same object. The Spanish team then checked with the IAU's Minor Planet Center which confirmed there was no record of the object. In an effort to establish priority, they emailed the MPC with their discovery on the night of 27 July. They did not mention the CalTech logs. Acknowledging that as a scientist he cannot not disprove their claims, Brown suggests that the Spanish team had improperly accessed information regarding where the CalTech team's telescope was pointed.

For our purposes, the question remains—how did Haumea get her name? Brown had initially suggested Santa. The name "Haumea" had apparently been proposed by David Rabinowitz of the Cal-Tech team on the basis that its planetary surface was almost entirely composed of rock. He reasoned that as a goddess of earth, Haumea is associated with rock and stone; hence, Haumea. It was later determined that while its interior was composed of rock, Haumea's outer shell is actually "nothing but ice." It is also noteworthy that the Spanish team had proposed that the dwarf planet be named "Ataecina." Ataecina was a goddess of the Iberian peninsula, associated with Persephone, the daughter of Ceres, who lived half the year with her mother and half the year with Hades-Pluto. The fact that the IAU adopted "Haumea," lends credence to Cal-Tech's claim of discovery, but contrary to usual practice, its official announcement of the discovery omits any reference about who discovered it. [297]

As opposed to Uranus, Neptune, Pluto and possibly Chiron, the designation of Haumea does not appear to coincide with significant global events. The number of other celestial bodies that have been discovered since the 1990's similarly precludes any tie-in predicated on that basis. These entities now number in the millions. [298] That deficiency has not, however, prevented their routine use as astrological significators on a par with the modern, as well as classical planets. The absence of a clear correlation between Haumea and world-wide movements, or the fact her naming fails to be supported by long-standing consensus, does not mean that the award of astrological significance should automatically be withdrawn, but rather, that we should make greater efforts to determine what we are really dealing with.

❧—⚍—❧

An Unexpected Consequence Of Celestial Proliferation

Although problems with attaining astrological legitimacy via the naming processes surrounding recently discovered celestial bodies have been amply demonstrated, let us assume they are unrelated to astrological analysis. At that point, all celestial bodies enjoy astrological significance. Software developers and glyph designers can rest easy with their latest versions. But the problem of numerosity looms: what do we do with the extraordinary volume of astrologically significant celestial entities? Faced with this dilemma, it is important to recognize a novel, and troublesome, feature of contemporary astrological interpretation. Without any benchmark or semblance of consensus, we find ourselves *picking and choosing* astrological significators independently and at will. *The problem highlighted here is not only <u>how</u> celestial bodies should be interpreted, but selecting <u>which</u> significator to use.* This dilemma represents a sea change in astrological practice. Traditional and modern astrologers had it easy—they utilized a modest number of planetary significators and examined all of them. To be sure, there are differences in emphasis and astrologers have never reached unanimity about each and every planetary characteristic, but one did not decide <u>whether</u> to look at Jupiter or the Moon. Today, one astrologer uses Lilith, while another may opt for Sedna or the Galactic Center.

If there is such a thing as the craft, practice or profession of astrology, then there must be a body of general principles that define it. While intuition and synchronicity inform our interpretations, these methods of understanding are also based on a set of guideposts that provide us vocabulary, syntax and punctuation points. One cannot, for example, play chess if one eliminates the queen or castles, or practice astrology if each astrologer decides what astrology is. Flexibility is one thing, but choosing astrological significators on a whim is another. We may be understandably reluctant to adopt a one-size-fits-all rulebook about how to approach celestial entities, but lumping everything into an astrologically significant category is not the answer either. Doing so intrinsically leeches meaning from the concept. If everything is significant, nothing is significant.

Picking and Choosing

The following outlines some considerations that may prove fruitful in moving beyond a "pick and choose" method of bestowing astrological significance. They are formatted as a series of questions rather than proposed answers, but as we know, framing the questions is often more important than providing the answers. They represent an attempt to weave astronomical knowledge into astrological expertise, much as the ancients did when they articulated their intimate connection between earth and sky.

1. Determination of Astrological Significance: As a general matter—are there newly discovered celestial entities which should generally be seen as connoting astrological significance, and others not? What kind of process might be employed in order to make this type of determination? How can intuition and flexibility be maintained without allowing astrological significance to go "all over the map?" What about such entities as moons or satellites, such as Jupiter's Ganymeade and Saturn's Titan which are both larger than Mercury? Should the presence of galactic reference points such as the Galactic Center and Anti-Center suggest astrological examination? Why, or why not? Are we ascribing heightened significance to Ceres, Pallas, Juno and Vesta because they

were the first to be named after Uranus and
before a number of other asteroids were discovered, or because it is now astrologically politically correct to do so?

2. Specific Celestial Body Features: In assessing
astrological significance, are some celestial
body features more or less relevant? Should
more attention be paid to planetary compo-
sition, such as ice versus rock versus gas, or
the nature of the ice, rock or gas? Ice can be
made of water as well as methane, for example. Other possible features include the shape
of the celestial body, whether other asteroids
are affiliated with it or whether it represents
fragments from another, larger body. The rotational speed, relative age or color as defined
by spectral class of the body might also be
considered. What axis or axes, or other mathematical points, might amplify our interpretations, particularly as we need not necessarily be limited to lunar or heliocentric nodes?

3. Groups or Classifications of Celestial Bodies:
Are there groups or classifications of planetary bodies that are more or less appropriate for use? Should we distinguish between
the Centaurs, Hildas and Trojans, or stars,
constellations, nebulae? Is there an inherent
astrological distinction between planets as a
group or collection of celestial entities and
the Galactic Center? What would a process

look like which attempts to deal with these issues? We speak of "personal," "social" and "outer" planets. Should we then have "outer-outer" and "beyond-outer" classifications? In examining this issue, it is not as if a bright line separates classical or modern planetary characteristics from another, and many times it is the interrelationship of these energies which is "where the action is."

4. Tying Planetary Bodies to a General Issue: Should certain celestial bodies, or groups of such bodies, be routinely considered when they relate to a particular issue, such as using Neptune, black holes, quasars and other anomalies when assessing a potential for inspiration or metaphysical sensitivities? Should Lilith be considered when a client presents with child abuse or adoption-related issues? Do we use a planetary body such as Eris when considering a feisty or combative Mars placement?

5. Ranking: Although there are considerable reasons to refrain from a process which ranks celestial significance, in the spirit of leaving no stone unturned, would it be appropriate to establish a system for ranking individual or groups of planetary bodies? For example, we may determine that the "personal" and "social" planets trump dwarf planets, which may in turn overshadow the Centaurs. Ad-

mittedly, the word "trump" may be a strong word, and the heart of a good astrological delineation lies in recognizing underlying patterns rather than setting up a hierarchy. On the other hand, how do we assess the relative weight of astrological indicators? Do we factor in astronomical measures such as planetary gravity and mass, rotational speed, magnitude, density or diameter? Adopting these measures may result in some rather unusual juxtapositions, however. For example, the gas giant Saturn is so light when compared to water that if we could obtain a basin big enough, it would float. That would then place Saturn at the bottom of the heap. [299] On that same scale, Charon, a satellite of Pluto, would outrank even Jupiter.

6. Outer-Outer Planets as Octaves: This consideration raises similar questions as those regarding ranking, but it is sufficiently different so as to merit separate consideration. Is it appropriate for astrologers to define a given issue, perhaps from a classical, ecliptic-based perspective, and then look to the newly discovered planetary bodies, including stellar and constellational information, to refine the issue? Do the Post-Plutonian planets provide levels, nuances or octaves of meaning? This analysis does not replicate John Addey's theory of harmonics, although his underlying

paradigm may provide guidance in answering these questions. Examples of this kind of analysis may suggest that Makemake represents a higher or particular octave of Mercury, or Ceto is an entity with something of Neptunian cast that might aid in understanding confusion, addiction.

7. Aspects / Declination: Might certain aspects be more relevant with certain planetary bodies? How might classical, outer and Post-Plutonian celestial entities cluster? How far into stellar space above and below the ecliptic or horizon should we go in assessing celestial relationships? One wonders what aspects to the Galactic Center or black holes might connote, or the *yana phuyu* or "black clouds" that Mayan astrologers recognized. [300] Again borrowing from Mayan cosmology, are there specific cycles, or cycles within cycles, that might inject a multi-layered or more dynamic platform for astrological analysis?

8. Personal, Subjective Affinity of the Astrologer—Is it a good idea to simply choose our own favorite prognosticators based on what we as astrologers most readily understand and resonate with? Is doing so the same thing as relying on a significator that we have experienced as being reliable in the past? These questions go to the very heart of the matter at hand and may dwarf the significance of any

of the above "picking and choosing" pitfalls. It is also no accident that they evoke Einstein's "observer bias" or Heisenberg's "uncertainty principle," not to mention Freudian "countertransference." Many of us may recognize the "transference" concept, but it is important to emphasize that countertransference is a process whereby a therapist's reactions can be related to the therapist's *own unconscious* thoughts and feelings, and not necessarily the content of their patients' reports. [301] Whether we like it or not, we navigate our lives with conscious and unconscious biases. These can be historical, cultural, familial, emotional, intellectual and so on. The problem, of course, is that the nature of a bias makes it difficult to perceive. Many of us are aware of the need to examine our own thoughts and feelings about a particular client, but we may not realize that unless we more carefully attend to the matter of picking and choosing significators, we may be choosing astrological tools dictated by other, more subtle and unconscious biases.

There is another level to the problem of an astrologer's subjective affinities in choosing significators and, I hope, it is one that astrologers are uniquely equipped to appreciate. It may also be what Post-Pluto is asking us to ponder. In addition to the biases noted above, our choices are also profoundly affected by astrological and karmic influences. At its most simplistic level, an astrologer with a Scorpio Ascendant or an abundance of Pluto in his or her chart may more fully appreciate the power of Lilith, someone with an Pisces Ascendant or a lot of Jupiter in his or her chart may resonate more fully with the Galactic Center, or a Gemini or Virgo emphasis may portend a reluctance to use any non-planets until sufficient proof of their relevance is established. We are also fortunate to have some guidance in parsing these profoundly meaningful influences: the knowledge imparted by astrology and our natal chart. The inevitable impact of these influences does not doom significator choices, and may in fact inform them. However, given the breadth of their ambit, we need to be as aware of them as we can when elucidating a significator.

Although undeniably important, we will not likely satisfy the challenges posed by the proliferation of celestial bodies by sequentially answering some or all of these questions. Were we to do so, we would not only become negatively attached to data collection, but more importantly, we would miss tasting the profound richness of the astrological feast that beckons us. We would also be dismissing the kind of messages offered by Post-Pluto, which augur the re-emergence of greater cosmological consciousness. Nor should we dismiss the knowledge imparted by modern science and astronomy. [302] The answer is not to supplant astrology with astronomy, but to acknowledge and incorporate astronomical discoveries without losing sight of the cosmological unity that makes the exercise meaningful in the first place.

A First Step In Finding Solutions—Sky Watching with Different Lenses

In attempting to navigate the astrological nexus, it will be wise for each of us to assess the strengths and limitations of the astrological perspectives that are familiar, as well as those that are not. Each astrological perspective undeniably offers a different slice or view of the cosmos, and each has value and can inspire a deeper understanding of our universe. Unfortunately, today's proponents of each approach segregate themselves by identifying with separate camps—or sky sectors. One approach uses a *tropically demarcated zodiacal ecliptic*. *Heliocentric* and *sidereal* approaches cull data from different perspectives, and there is also a *constellational* point of view. There are other frameworks as well, some of which represent versions of one or another of these models and others that are markedly different. Each of these approaches or "measuring sticks" will invariably shape our perception of cosmos and is inextricably related to the questions it asks and how it determines what has meaning. Whether by emphasis or content, data is selected and information is derived on the basis of a given model's goals. Too often, information flows from the goalpost to the data, and not the other way around. This problem is exacerbated by many astrologers who use the perspective that initially introduced them to astrology and electing not to investigate others. We should instead be thinking about what works (or not) in what circumstances, and why (or why not) it works. As might be expected with a Post-Pluto paradigm, multiple astrological frames of reference may be of particular relevance when analyzing multiple astronomically derived data sets. Post-Pluto also seems to emphasize inter-planetary processes, such as synodic connections or eclipses, rather than cataloguing astronomical data for each celestial entity or group of celestial entities. By walking in the shoes of each perspective, it is as if we are travelling to another country or connecting with a culture other than our own. It is not simply that we eat different foods or learn about a different history or architecture, but that we come to learn about *ourselves* and *our* culture. And our astrology.

Multiple Astrological Perspectives: A Post-Plutonian Network

Unpacking astronomical data from each perspective is important, but shuffling and re-packing that deck has the potential to generate a more inclusive and dynamic picture. Realizing that each perspective reveals different facets of the astrological prism may allow us to more fully evaluate the impact of newly discovered bodies upon our craft. For example, the relative and real brightness of a celestial body has fascinating implications. It highlights how fast or bright celestial energy *seems to be* versus *what actually it is*—thus, the intriguing interplay of appearances and reality. One can even ponder the implications of the fact that a celestial body is maximally bright when it is at its greatest distance from the Sun, yet maximally close to Earth. Or, if a particular planet seems to dominate a chart drawn with the tropical ecliptic model, it might also be important to observe the path the planet is tracing vis-à-vis the Earth, the Sun and/or stars, or its synodic connections with these bodies. If we emphasize cycles rather than rely solely on flash-freeze celestial points, relationships between stars and new celestial bodies may generate new potentials for multi-layered meaning. For example, when a celestial body is perceived from Earth as moving backwards (retrograde), what is happening to its heliocentric position or its proximity to Aldebaran? What might the impact be between a planet aspecting a star when either celestial body becomes visible above the eastern horizon, after not having been visible for a while (heliacal rising)? What kinds of energies come and go, or what stories may be told about these circumstances?

As we know, our ancestors made a veritable host of sky observations and a number of modern astrologers have revived their practices. According to the late astrologer Diana K. Rosenberg, it is important to consider not only stars and constellations on the ecliptic, but also "those of the *Sphaera Barbarica*—the figures above and below the ecliptic—even those very far from it, near the poles. [303] A star's size, magnitude and nearness to the ecliptic do not necessarily limit their impact because some "very dim stars, far from the ecliptic, pack quite a wallop!" [304] Bernadette Brady articulates a compelling example of a star-based point of view in her exposition of Visual Astrology. [305] A central proposition of this model lies in her assertion that astrologers need not be wedded to the ecliptic. She agrees that Ptolemy's ecliptic-based mathematics may have provided a more efficient and accessible manner by which to identify planetary positions in that astronomers could mark celestial placements with the precision of a standardized zodiacal degree (e.g. Mars or Aldebaran at 9° Gemini). By doing so, however, Brady contends that our celestial sphere became relegated to a two-dimensional line, ejecting sky objects from their constellational homes and depriving them of their integrity. She states,

> "The sky is not a single line, the ecliptic, but a great dome of wonder that surrounds us, wrapping us in a cloak of mythology, stories and constant narratives. I personally do not want to be limited to the shoelace of the ecliptic as my only contact with the sky; I want to experience the wonder of the heavens in their entirety." [306]

In his book on *The Light of Venus*, astrologer Adam Gainsburg demonstrates how spending time looking up and informing oneself about the visible sky can expand our understanding of a celestial body's astrological significance. [307] Instead of relying on a zodiacal ecliptic grid, Gainsburg highlights a planet's phase, or ". . . the dynamic sub-section of its complete cycle with another body—[that] conveys a broader message than the planet by itself." [308] Some of the many parameters he uses in exploring Venus include its visibility, sky appearance (morning or evening star), real-time speed, heliacal rising and setting times, magnitude (relative brightness), retrograde status and elongation (longitude). Each phase in the cycle is expressed by a combination of these features so that, for example, Venus displays two periods of invisibility: one when she is closest to Earth and moving retrograde, and the other when she is furthest from Earth and moving direct. He marks whether Venus makes a morning or evening appearance, and how bright it is when visible. By observing the sky in this manner and applying his observations in client practice, Gainsburg is able to hypothesize that an invisible Venus "sensitizes you to the energy or dynamics with others and encourages stronger reliance on your inner life." Increasing brightness lends "confidence, optimism or naiveté that your efforts will have a positive impact." Venus at its furthest from the rising Sun "strengthens your drive to align your life with your desires." Gainsburg expands his "whole sky" analysis to other planets as well. [309] For example, in focusing on the heliacal cycles, he suggests that those planets that appear before sunrise in the Eastern sky "operate from a *Subjective* context," and function through "an underlying orientation of 'I-Me-Mine' or 'Sovereignty of Self' perspective." Evening Sky planets "operate from an *Objective* context," and function through "an underlying orientation of mutuality or the 'Us-We,' the 'Mutuality of We' perspective." This does not mean that planets rising after sunrise are selfish, or those appearing after sunset are expansive, but these descriptions indicate an essential orientation or starting point. As we can see, Gainsburg has employed information from more than one perspective in order to more fully explicate astrological significance.

In attempting to delineate astrologically relevant astronomical information, one of the first activities we can undertake is to look *up* at the sky. Or, to look at the cosmos with eyes as the ancients did, with eyes unfettered by frameworks and perspectives. To be sure, nowadays we cannot sit on our back porches and trace all celestial movements in the same fashion or with the same clarity as our forebears followed the "wanderers," but I daresay that many astrologers have not taken the time to establish direct connection with celestial entities that are visible with the naked eye, or experience the sensitive points of the zodiac beyond our local solar system. We need to do so. Once we have embarked on this visual journey, we can look AROUND the cosmological expanse with all the tools that contemporary science offers us. If

we demur, we conspire to foster continuing discon-
nection and estrangement from the cosmos' heart-
song. As Bernadette Brady importunes, astrologers
can fully experience the starry night sky, "allowing it
a place in their astrological souls."[310] We can then use
these observations, working from the "ground up."

Conclusion

❧ — ⋘⋙ — ❧

The Opportunity for Astrological Reaffirmation

Grappling with the appearance of newly discovered objects inaugurates a journey of re-acquaintance with the cosmos. The sky is indeed trying to tell us something, and we would be woefully remiss if we fail to heed its messages. In embarking on this journey, we have an opportunity to re-examine the nexus between astrology and astronomy, as well as the underlying *logos* that supports our craft. This involves not only addressing the naming of celestial objects, but the fundamental message imparted by the appearance of so many at this moment in time. And, importantly, to use an astrological lens when doing so. Our approach should not be one designed to compete with or outshine our astronomical colleagues, but to demonstrate that we offer a genuine path to deeper understanding of the cosmos. We can make some headway in meeting this challenge by acknowledging and becoming familiar with the questions posed by our newly re-defined solar system and the astrological frameworks discussed above. However, as if these challenges were not sufficiently daunting, undertaking this journey immediately highlights another series of questions that go to the very heart of astrology. Simply stated—what is, or should be, an astrologer's role? What does astrology seek to reveal? Who or what is our clientele? Are we psychological counselors, spiritual healers or agents of spiritual transcendence / transformation, evaluators of the state of global consciousness and/or world affairs, metaphysicians, financial advisors, researchers, historians, software designers, publicists? Before deciding which celestial entities to use, we need to think about the broader picture: what we are doing when we use significators or sensitive points? These are not questions of methodology or taxonomy, but cosmological ontology. There is likely—and hopefully—no one answer to these questions, but without serious examination, we may find ourselves heading off into so many directions that at the end of the day, we can't find each other.

Perhaps astrologers are being asked to meet the challenge of the adage, "be careful what you wish for." For such a long time astrology has been derided and shunned, and we are now enjoying a welcome resurgence of interest in and use of astrology. [311] On the other hand, we need to stop and consider where we are taking astrology and where astrology is taking us. The extraordinary diversity of contemporary astrological goals and ambitions is difficult to miss. One need only point to the wide-ranging nature of workshop tracks that were offered at the 2012 United Astrology Conference. [312] It is instructive to peruse the wide-ranging variety of astrological objectives that were articulated in just one of these tracks—the Esoteric /Philosophical /Spiritual track. In their presentation within this module, Steven Forrest and Robert Mulligan sought to support the "spiritual growth and inner lives of individuals." The introductory material for this track advised that the subjects to be covered included the Kabbalah, theosophy, Hinduism, Buddhism, evolutionary astrology, reincarnation, meditation, and Hermetic traditions. Within that same track, Alan Oken spoke of "the astrologer as healer," Laura Nalbandian described how Uranus and trauma can serve as liberating forces, and Marguerite dar Boggia presented her work on the nature of energy. I do not for a moment disparage the informative quality of any of these presentations, or the soul-level integrity of the presenters, and indeed I wish I could have attended every one of these lectures. On the other hand, I have some concern that we will devolve into a rudder-less compendium of different points of view regarding the role of astrology. The problem of independently "picking and choosing" significators that plagues the incorporation of newly discovered celestial bodies into our charts is also mirrored in the divergence of goals astrologers currently espouse. If one is tempted to say, "all of the above" in response to the iteration of the many roles astrologers can assume, and without some level of reflection, we may lose our bearings and bypass the essential truths that have kept astrology as vital as it is.

Post Quantum Astrology—
As Around, So Within

The bad news is that it looks as if change is here to stay, but the good news, of course, is that it looks as if change is here to stay. I most sincerely hope that our response to the massive planetary proliferation does not trigger another astrological exit. As astrologers, we have a unique opportunity to discern profound seeds of growth within the embrace of cosmological wisdom. As the contextual psychologist Stephen Hayes importunes,

> "Living traditions should never allow themselves to become monuments to what was— they are postures toward . . . what can be."[313]

In the same vein and as earlier discussed regarding the naming processes surrounding post-classical planets, there is a meaning to this celestial abundance, which is greater than the sum of its various parts. Neptune, Uranus and Pluto sought to direct our attention to global events and movements that signaled worldwide social, economic and political changes. Pluto's demotion redefined what it meant to be a "planet" and thereby signaled the opening of the floodgates to new celestial paradigm. Importantly, this reclassification also exposed the fallacy of humanity's efforts to superimpose limits, while at the same time underscoring the message that humans and the universe participate in creation within an all-encompassing web of interconnectedness.

Let us also give the Post-Pluto and Uranus square its due. Astronomers have much to learn from astrologers, and we astrologers have much to learn from each other. It is time to dig in on many levels and for astrologers, not astronomers, to develop an astrology that advances our truth. To demonstrate an ability to take perspectives that may seem mutually exclusive of other perspectives, and bind them to the wisdom of sky consciousness that informed the ancients and beckons to us today. By doing so, we will reveal another level of cosmological compassion—to reach around and within. As the main characters in the recent Home Box Office production *True Detective* acknowledge,

> Rust Cohle: "It's the first story, the oldest."
> Marty Hart: "What's that?"
> RC: "Light versus dark."
> MH: "Well, I know it ain't Alaska but it appears to me the dark has a lot more territory."

RC: "You're looking at it wrong, this sky thing."
MC: "How's that?"
RC: "Once there was only dark. You ask me, the light's winnin'." [314]

NOTES

1   Terence Dickinson, Hubble's Universe: Greatest Discoveries and Latest Images, Firefly Books: Buffalo, NY, 2012, p. 21.

2   James Herschel, Holden, MA, FAFA, A History of Horoscopic Astrology: From the Babylonian Period to the Modern Age, 2nd ed, American Federation of Astrologers: Tempe, AZ, 2006, p. 234.

3   Alan Stern, PhD, astrophysicist and principal investigator for the New Horizons mission to Pluto, presents a fascinating UTube video describing this revolution: http://www.youtube.com/watch?v=8Nk2LF22W64. See also, Michael E. Brown, PhD, How I Killed Pluto and Why It Had It Coming, Spiegel & Grau: New York, reprint edition, 2012, pp. 27-28. Michael Brown is the Richard and Barbara Rosenberg Professor of Planetary Astronomy at the California Institute of Technology. More information regarding Brown can be found at http://www.gps.caltech.edu/~mbrown/bio.html. He is best known for his discovery of Eris, as well as his "almost" discovery of Haumea discussed more fully below. He has also published numerous articles regarding newly discovered celestial bodies, which are not only informative, but often display a refreshingly wry sense of humor.

4   Robert Hand, "Why Is It So Difficult to Prove Astrology?" This is a lecture given by Hand at a Northern Oregon and Washington Astrology conference, May 2012.

5   Bernadette Brady, Introductory Lecture on Visual Astrology given at the October, 2005 Conference of the Astrological Association of Great Britain, York, UK.

6   I am an astrological beginner or, perhaps more accurately – an astrological intermediate. The disadvantage of this status is that I still have incredible amounts of astrology to learn and, often at the most inconvenient times, experience lacunae in my still-growing store of astrological knowledge. The advantage is that I am not necessarily encumbered with an astrological perspective I have used for years and years. I have consummate respect for astrological scholarship, and often challenge people who are dubious about astrology's merits to attend a regional or national conference. I can only hope that the thoughts I offer here will further illuminate the tantalizing penumbra that surrounds the wisdom known as astrology.

7   The designation "pluton" is geological and refers to a type of igneous or volcanic rock. I refer the reader to Wikipedia or other sources, as this is a field about which I know nothing. A plutoid is a trans-Neptunian object and a plutino is a type of plutoid. An orbital resonance of 2:3 means that for every two orbits a given celestial body makes, another celestial body makes three.

8   The official site for this designation can be found at: http://www.iau.org/public_press/news/detail/iau0804/. Some sound explanations and a critique of IAU's definitions are made by Michael E. Brown's article on "The Dwarf Plan-

ets" available at http://web.gps.caltech.edu/~mbrown/dwarfplanets/.

9   The IAU draft definition of "planet" and "plutons"(Press release). International Astronomical Union. 2006-08-16, at http://www.iau.org/public_press/news/detail/iau0601/.

10   See, Alex Fileppenko, PhD, Professor of Astronomy at the University of California, Berkeley, in the Guidebook accompanying the compact disc presentation Understanding the Universe: An Introduction to Astronomy, 2nd Edition, The Teaching Company, 2007, at pp. 176-180 of Lecture Thirty-Four: "Asteroids and Dwarf Planets." See also, Michael E. Brown (2006). "The Eight Planets". *Caltech*. Retrieved 2007-02-21.at http://web.gps.caltech.edu/~mbrown/eightplanets.

11   Id.

12   See, additional information from Michael E. Brown at http://www.mikebrownsplanets.com/2008/06/ground-rules-for-debating-definiton-of.html.

13   Citation is from "The Eight Planets" by Michael E. Brown cited above, p. 2.

14   See, "IAU Resolution B5: Pluto," available at: http://www.iau.org/static/resolutions/Resolution_GA26-5-6.pdf.

15   This is proposed by Professor Filippenko at p. 179 of the Understanding the Universe Guidebook, cited above.

16   Michael E. Brown, http://www.gps.caltech.edu/~mbrown/dps.html - In this article Brown posts an article dated 9 January 2014, which speaks to the question of dwarf planets. He states that there are 10 objects which "are nearly certainly" dwarf planets, 23 objects which are "highly likely" to be dwarf planets, 45 objects which are "likely"

to be dwarf planets, 78 objects which are "probably" dwarf planets and 339 objects which are "possibly" dwarf planets.

17   Eric Hand, "Astronomers Say a Neptune-sized planet lurks beyond Pluto," Science, January, 2016. As might be anticipated, one of the astronomers making this discovery is Michael Brown. The other is Konstantin Batygin, Assisatant Professor of Planetary Science at the California Institute of Technology. As to naming, they are calling it "Planet Nine," although "Planet Phattie," which is apparently 1990's slang for "cool." See, Batygin and Brown, "Evidence for a Distant Giant Planet in the Solar System," The Astronomical Journal, January 20, 2016, Abstract available at http://iopscience.iop.org/article/10.3847/0004-6256/151/2/22/meta.

18   See, e.g., http://science.nasa.gov/science-news/science-at-nasa/2013/29may_asteroidfamilies/.

19   Maria Cruz and Robert Coontz, "Alien Worlds Galore," Science, Vol. 340, 3 May 2013, p. 565, available at http://science.sciencemag.org/content/340/6132/565.full.

20   See Michael E. Brown at http://discovermagazine.com/2006/may/cover#.UnFACpFDI9Y.

21   Alicia Chang, "Smallest Planet Yet Found Outside the Solar System," Nation, 21 February 2013. The article's "jelly beans" quotation came from Geoff Marcy, PhD, the University of California, Berkeley astronomer who discovered numerous extra-solar planets . The celestial body referred to in the article is Kepler 37b, a star that orbits 210 light years away in constellation Lyra. It was discovered by Thomas Barclay of NASA Ames Research Center

in Northern California. See also, http://www.nasa.gov/mission_pages/kepler/news/kepler-37b.html.

22   See, Mike E. Brown's article at http://www.mikebrowns-planets.com/2009/08/planetary-placemats.html.

23   Demetra George, MA, "Asteroids and Mythic Astrology (June 2010)," at http://www.demetra-george.com/Asteroids_Mythic_Astrology.pdf article.

24   Id. at p. 1.

25   See Daniel J. Siegel, PhD, <u>The Developing Mind: Toward a Neurobiology of Interpersonal Experience</u>, Guilford Press: New York, 1999; Joseph LeDoux, PhD, <u>The Emotional Brain: The Mysterious Underpinnings of Emotional Life</u>, Touchstone: New York, 1996; Antonio Damasio, PhD, <u>The Feeling of What Happens: Body and Emotion in the Making of Consciousness</u>, Harcourt: San Diego, 1999.

26   See, "Rule-governed behavior," Relational Frame Theory, <u>http://relationalframetheory.wikispaces.com/Rule-governed+behavior</u>. This wiki is described as: ". . . a knowledge base for those learning RFT (Hayes, S.C., Barnes-Holmes, D., & Roche, 2001, and Torneke, 2010). Relational frame theory, or RFT, is a psychological theory of human language and cognition, based on the philosophical roots of functional contextualism. In other words, RFT is a behavioral and empirical approach to language and cognition."

27   Philip K. Dick, "How to Build a Universe That Doesn't' Fall Apart Two Days Later," 1978, at http://deoxy.org/pkd_how2build.htm.

28   Demetra George and Douglas Bloch, <u>Asteroid God-desses: the Mythology, Psychology, and Astrology of the Re-Emerging Feminine</u>, Ibis Press: Lake Worth, Florida, 2003.

29   Liz Greene, "The Academy as an Archetypal Group Dynamic, in Astrology and the Academy," Papers from the Inaugural Conference of the Sophia Centre, Bath Spa University College, 13-14 June, 2003, ed. Nicholas Campion, Patrick Curry and Michael York, Cinnabar Books: Bristol, 2004, pp. 90-102, at p. 102. Ms. Greene is a well-known astrologer, psychologist and author.

30   Robert Hand, <u>Horoscope Symbols</u>, Whitford Press: Atglen, PA, 1981, p, 22

31   Athony Aveni, PhD, <u>Stairways to the Stars: Skywatching in Three Ancient Cultures</u>, John Wiley & Sons: Canada; 1997, p. 37.

32   Bernadette Brady, Astrology, <u>A Place in Chaos</u>, The Wessex Astrologer Ltd: Bournemouth, England, 2006, p. 17.

33   Robert Hand, <u>Chronology of Astrology of the Middle East and the West by Period</u>, 2d ed, Archive for the Retrieval of Historical Astrological Texts (ARHAT): Reston, VA, 2008; See also, Nicholas Campion, <u>A History of Western Astrology Volume 1: The Ancient and Classical Worlds</u>, Continuum International Publishing Group: London, 2008, p. 7.

34   See Jack Phillips, "'Oldest' Calendar Discovered in Aberdeenshire, Scotland, <u>Epoch Times</u>, 15 July 2013, available at <u>http://www.theepochtimes.com/n3/179232-oldest-calendar-discovered-in-aberdeenshire-scotland/</u>.

35   Anthony Aveni, <u>People and the Sky: Our Ancestors and the Cosmos</u>, Thames & Hudson: New York NY, 2008, p. 137.

36   Francesca Rochberg, PhD, <u>The Heavenly Writing: Divination, Horoscopy, and Astronomy in Mesopotamian Culture</u>, Cambridge University Press: Cambridge, MA, 2004, pp. 4, 7. Nicholas Campion, <u>A History of Western Astrology: Vol. I</u>, cited above, p. 69. The dates cited here reflect a more or less final version of these texts, but the observations extend considerably before. Professor Rochberg is a historian of science who is a Professor of Near Eastern Studies at the University of California, Berkeley.

37   Francesca Rochberg, <u>The Heavenly Writing</u>, p. 24.

38   A heliacal rising takes place when a celestial body is first visible in the Eastern horizon before the Sun rises after the period when it was not visible. See also, Rochberg, <u>The Heavenly Writing</u>, p. 24.

39   Francesca Rochberg, <u>The Heavenly Writing</u>, p. 24; Robert Powell, <u>The History of the Zodiac</u>, Sophia Academic Press: San Rafael, CA, 2007, p. 109; Kenneth Bowser, <u>An Introduction to Western Sidereal Astrology</u>, American Federation of Astrologers, Inc.: Tempe AZ, 2012, p. 186.

40   Francesca Rochberg, <u>The Heavenly Writing</u>, pp. 127-128, footnote 21.

41   Id. p. 6.

42   Id. pp. 26, 110-114, 138-140, 275.

43   Gerd Grabhoff, "Normal Star Observations in Late Astronomical Babylonian Deities," <u>Ancient Astronomy and Celestial Divination</u>, edited by N.M. Swerdlow, PhD, The MIT Press: Cambridge MA, 1999, pp. 97 – 147.

44   Nicholas Campion, <u>A History of Western Astrology: Volume 1</u>, pp. 181-182, 209; Powell, <u>The History of the Zodiac</u>, pp. 19-20.

45   Robert Powell, <u>The History of the Zodiac</u>, pp. 17-18; International Astronomical Union, "The Constellations: Origin of the Constellations," available at: http://www.iau.org/public/themes/constellations.

46   Nicholas Campion, <u>A History of Western Astrology: Volume 1</u>, p. 23

47   Id. pp. 20-21.

48   Id. p. 12.

49   N.M. Swerdow, "Introduction," in <u>Ancient Astronomy and Celestial Divination</u>, cited above, p. 1.

50   Nicholas Campion argues that in Mesopotamian culture astrology's capacity to predict was subsidiary to its attempts to heal the rift between the immutable order of the universe, as against the spontaneous manipulations of the gods. <u>A History of Western Astrology: Volume 1</u>, p. 42. Astrology was therefore "a means of exploiting this uncertainty in order to better manage the future." While entirely apt, this distinction or the fact that it represents a kind of divination does not contradict the part prediction played in Mesopotamian astrology. The difference lies more clearly in the method of or path to prediction than a denial that prediction constituted an important part of Mesopotamian astrology; The creation of the *Enuma Anu Enlil* took place over a long period of time, from ca. 2000 BCE until the 7th century BCE when it was canonized during the reign of King Esarhaddon (680-669 BCE) and Assurbanipal (668-627 BCE). Francesca Rochberg, <u>The</u>

Heavenly Writing, cited above, pp. 4-6. The astronomical date of the Venus Tablet of *Ammisaduqa* date to 1646-1626 BCE, the date of the beginning of the First Babylonian dynasty. At p. 75. Except where I believe it may be particularly helpful, I have not placed quotation marks around all of the factual references to *Enuma Anu Enlil*, but they are entirely taken from Rochberg's The Heavenly Writing, cited above. My scholarship is limited to having read the results of her impressive scholarship.

51   Bernadette Brady, Astrology, A Place in Chaos, p. 18; Campion, A History of Western Astrology: Volume I, pp. 61-62.

52   Francesca Rochberg, The Heavenly Writing, p. 67.

53   In evaluating the predictive value of the royal omens, I am reminded of First Lady Nancy Reagan's consultation with astrologer Joan Quigley and her apparent influence on the timing of President Reagan's decisions. See, What Does Joan Say?: My Seven Years as White House Astrologer to Nancy and Ronald Reagan, Carol Publishing Group: New York, 1990.

54   Nicholas Campion, A History of Western Astrology: Volume I, p. 62, footnote 39, citing Erica Reiner and David Pingree, Babylonian Planetary Omens, Part 3 (Styx Publications: Groningen, 1998), p. 43 (Omens 28, 31, 55).

55   Nicholas Campion, A History of Western Astrology: Volume I, p. 81, footnote 53, citing Henri Frankfort, Kingship and the Gods: A Study of Near Eastern Religion as Integration of Society and Nature, Chicago University Press: Chicago IL, 1978 [1948].

56   Francesca Rochberg, The Heavenly Writing, p 204.

57   Id. p. 58-59. Rochberg generally divides omens into two categories: those that are (1) "provoked" and represent "messages from gods in response to questions posed to them by various methods of manipulator by the diviner," and (2) "unprovoked" which are "simply observed without a specific request for he appearance of a sign from the deity," p. 47. Admittedly, 21st century astrologers do not by and large explicitly engage in divinatory practices. This said, this ancient Babylonian practice is no less rational or logical, and was based on a solid record of continuous observations. Rochberg also provides more complex background for the genesis of the if-then format. It arose from a "particular scribal practice . . . in Sumerian lexical texts," whereby each entry, whether it was a "single sign, a compound sign, or several words" was given a single line. Scholarly divination texts followed this pattern whereby each new line was indicated by means of a vertical wedge. The adaptation of the vertical wedge to divinatory practice, "[i]nstead of indicating 'item,' or the like, it came to represent the first word of the omen formula 'if. . . . " pp. 52-53. See also, N.M. Swerdlow, The Babylonian Theory of the Planets, Princeton University Press: Princeton, NJ, 1998, pp. 3-4.

58   Id. pp. 58, 52-53; N.M. Swerdlow, "Introduction," in Ancient Astronomy and Celestial Divination, cited above, pp. 15.

59   Francesca Rochberg, The Heavenly Writing, p. 45-46.

60   Giorgio de Santillana and Hertha von Dechend, Hamlet's Mill: An Essay Investigating the Origin of Human Knowledge and Its Transmission Through Myth," first

paperback edition, David R. Godine: Jaffrey, NH, 1977; Giulio Magli, "Mathematics, Astronomy and Sacred Landscape in the Inka Heartland," Nexus Network Journal, Vol. 7, no. 2, Autumn, 2005, available at: http://www.nexusjournal.com/Magli.html.

61   Nicholas Campion, A History of Western Astrology: Volume I, cited above, p. 58.

62   Anthony Aveni, Stairways to the Stars: Skywatching in Three Ancient Cultures, cited above, p. 135.

63   Id. p. 98.

64   John Major Jenkins, Galactic Alignment: The Transformation of Consciousness According to Mayan, Egyptian and Vedic Traditions, Bear & Company: Rochester, Vermont, 2002.

65   Laeticia Grevers, "The Incan Milky Way: A Path to Another World," The Bolivian Express, 30 September, 2012, available at http://www.bolivianexpress.org/blog/posts/the-incan-milky-way.

66   Anthony Aveni, Stairways to the Stars, cited above, p. 49

67   Giulio Magli, PhD, "On the astronomical content of the sacred landscape of Cusco in Inka times," available at http://arxiv.org/pdf/physics/0408037.pdf.

68   See, e.g. Geoffrey Cornelius, The Moment of Astrology: Origins in Divination, The Wessex Astrology Ltd: Bournenouth, England, 2003. Cornelius concludes that astrology is essentially divinity, depending upon an "interpretive act." Id. p. 278.

69   Gary Phillipson, "An Interview with Robert Hand," taken from Phillipson's interview with Hand on 8 September

2002 at the Conference of the Astrological Association of Great Britain.

70   Id.

71   This reference may be obscure, but I cannot resist it. The words come from a song sung by Adoo Annie in Rodgers and Hammerstein's 1931 musical "Oklahoma."

72   Nicholas Campion, A History of Western Astrology: Volume I, p. 23.

73   Anthony Aveni, Stairway to the Stars, p. 83.

74   Nicholas Campion, A History of Western Astrology: Volume I, p. 18.

75   Anthony Aveni, Stairways to the Stars, p. 85.

76   Nicholas Campion, A History of Western Astrology: Volume I, p. 24.

77   Anthony Aveni, Stairways to the Stars, pp. 60-61. There is a recent article regarding the mound Maes Howe and the "complex of monumental buildings" in Orkney, Scotland in the August 2014 edition of National Geographic, "The First Stonehenge: Scotland's Master Builders," by Roff Smith and photographs by Jim Richardson, pp. 26-51. This site contains "one of the largest roofed structures built in prehistoric northern Europe." Smith cites archeologist Nick Card who states, "The people who built this thing had big ideas. There were out to make a statement." Id., p. 32. Much as the Mayan and Egyptian cultures, many of these iconic structures are also aligned in a manner that underscores this observation. Within a mile of each other are the stone circles known as The Ring of Brodgar and Stones of Stenness, and one mile away is Maes Howe whose ". . . entry passage is perfectly aligned to receive the

rays of the setting sun on the eve of the winter solstice, illuminating its inner chamber on the shortest day of the year." Id, p. 32

78   Anthony Aveni, <u>Stairways to the Stars</u>, p. 150-154.

79   Anthony Aveni, <u>People and the Sky</u>, p. 125.

80   Id. p. 124.

81   In examining ancient cultures and as discussed above, we must of course be cognizant that names impart reality, and we walk a very tight rope when attempting to comprehend the mindset and essential spirit of these early cultures. It is also beyond the purview of this article to fully delineate the discoveries of archeo-astronomy / astrology, but we would be remiss in failing to evaluate the paradigm that fertilized and incubated the study of the stars – particularly when recent astronomical discoveries place us at similar crossroads.

82   Giulio Magli, <u>Architecture, Astronomy and Sacred Landscape in Ancient Egypt</u>, Cambridge University Press: New York, 2013, pp. 20-21. Dr. Magli is a full professor of Mathematical Physics of the Faculty of Civil, Environmental and Land Planning at the Dipartimento di Matematica del Politecnico di Milano. He has also researched and written about the topic of archeoastronomy.

83   Bernadette Brady, <u>Astrology: A Place in Chaos</u>, cited above, p 14.

84   Id. p. 16.

85   Nicholas Campion, <u>Astrology and Cosmology In The World's Religions</u>, New York University Press: New York and London 2012, at p 6.

86   Bernadette Brady, <u>Astrology: A Place in Chaos</u>, p. 18.

87   See, e.g. Alexander Ruperti, <u>Cycles of Becoming: The Planetary Pattern of Growth</u>, Earthwalk School of Astrology: Santa Monica, CA, 2005, p. 3.

88   The Emerald Tablet of Hermes Trismegistus, <u>http://www.sacred-texts.com/alc/emerald.htm</u>; See also, Demetra George, <u>Asteroids and Mythic Astrology</u>, cited above, footnote #43, where she quotes from the Emerald Tablet: "What is below is like that which is above, and what is above is like that which is below, to accomplish the miracles of one thing."

89   Bernadette Brady, <u>Astrology: A Place in Chaos</u>, cited above, p. 37.

90   See, "Facts and Figures" sections regarding each planet, available at solarsystem.nasa/gov/planets/profile.

91   James Herschel Holden, <u>A History of Horoscopic Astrology: From the Babylonian Period to the Modern Age</u>, cited above, p. 13.

92   Nicholas Campion, <u>A History of Western Astrology: Volume I</u>, pp. 153, 218.

93   Carl G. Jung, <u>Man and His Symbols</u>, Aldus Books Ltd: London, 1964, pp. 66-67.

94   Carl G. Jung, <u>Man and His Symbols</u>, pp. 66-67.

95   A profound discussion of the affinities between metals and planetary identities is presented by Nicholas Kollerstrom, PhD, in "The Metal-Planet Affinities-The Sevenfold Pattern," available at: <u>http://www.alchemywebsite.com/kollerstrom_sevenfold.html</u>.

96   It is interesting to pick out the familiar symbols noted by Deborah Houlding, horary astrologer, author and sponsor of the informative website: <u>http://www.skyscript.co.uk</u> in

her article, "Charts and Symbols in Early Astrology: A study of the Chart form of L 597," available at http://www.skyscript.co.uk/greek_horoscope.html. In this article Houlding explores the "symbolic encoding of astrological information" in a Greek chart dated 478 CE. She has also made this endeavor quite user-friendly by allowing us to view the chart in the original Greek, as well as in an English transliteration and a computer reproduction. As she notes, most of the academic examination of early astrological charts has unfortunately tended to focus on the text rather than the accompanying diagrams.

97   Annie Scott Dill Maunder, "The Origin of the Symbols of the Planets, "The Observatory, NASA Astrophysics Data System, No. 723, August, 1934, 238-247.

98   Deborah Houlding, "Charts and Symbols in Early Astrology: A study of the chart form of L 497," cited above.

99   See, Jim A. Cornwell, "Translation of the Figures in the Zodiac of Denderah," in The Alpha and Omega, Chapter One, 1995, available in part at http://www.mazzaroth.com/ChapterOne/TranslateDenderah.htm

There remains some controversy about dating the Dendera ceiling, although Egyptologist Sylvia Cauville and astrophysicist Eric Aubourg conclude that the solar eclipse portrayed in the design occurred on 7 March 51 BCE and a lunar eclipse can be dated to 25 September 52 BCE at Dendera, Egypt. Cauville hypothesizes that the use of these dates reflects a desire on the part of the Egyptians who wished to commemorate the death of Cleopatra's father Ptolemy Aauletes whose death coincided with the total solar eclipse. See, Sylvia Cauville, Le Zodiaque d'Osiris, Uitgeverij Peeters: Bondgenotenlaan, Belgium, 1997.

100 See, e.g. (1) a number of fascinating and erudite works written by Robert Zollar, scholar of Medieval Astrology and proponent of Western Predictive Astrology, generally available at www.new-library.com. In particular, see: "The Occult Sciences of Astrology, Alchemy and Magic," 3rd electronic publication, New Library Limited: London, 2004, and "The Hermetic Tradition," 2nd electronic publication, New Library Limited: London 2004, and (2) gnosis.org, including the Reverend Stephan A. Hoeller, "On the Trail of the Winged God: Hermes and Hermeticism Throughout the Ages," which first appeared in Gnosis: A Journal of Western Inner Traditions (Vol. 40, Summer, 1996) and reproduced at http://www.gnosis.org/hermes.htm.

101 All the descriptive phrases, such as "Circle of Spirit," in this section are taken from Adam Gainsburg, Sacred Marriage Astrology: The Soul's Desire for Wholeness, Cold Tree Press: Nashville, TN, 2005, pp. 297-298. There is some additional information about glyphs available in A. T. Mann, The Round Art of Astrology: An Illustrated Guide to Theory and Practice, Vega Books: United Kingdom, 2003, pp. 83-84.

102 The references to alchemical metals in this section are taken from Lacquanna Paul & Robert Powell's Cosmic Dances of the Planets, Sophia Foundation Press: San Rafael CA, 2007, and Nicholas Kollerstrom, "The Metal Planet Affinities," cited above.

103 William Shakespeare, King John, Act IV, Scene 2.

104 The elongations relate to the points of greatest or maximum distance from the Sun.

105 Phyllis E. Johnson, David B. Milne and Glenn I. Lykken, "Effects of Age and Sex on Copper Absorption, Biological Half Life, and Status in Humans," available at http://naldc.nal.usda.gov/download/48292/PDF. "NALDC" refers to the United States Department of Agricultures National Agricultural Library.

106 When assessing the correlation between our Earthly observations of Mars and the Martian personality as is outlined here, I cannot help but take note of the apparent discovery that at one time Mars had enough water to form a very large ocean. See, Dirk Schulze-Makuch, "Mars Once Had an Ocean – A Big One," Air Space Magazine, 3-10-15; Dwayne Brown, Nancy N. Jones, and Elizabeth Zurbritsky, "NASA Research Suggests Mars Once Had More Water Than Earth's Arctic Ocean, 5 March 2015, available at the nasa.gov website. An abundance of water does not evoke our traditional understanding of Mars. What should the impact be, if any of this "actual" information? Do we rely on our "apparent" observations alone? If we choose this option, and because we generally cannot see beyond Saturn, does our query regarding celestial body proliferation end and our charts only include classical planets?

107 Darby Costello, "Ardour, Desire and Excellence," The Mars Quartet: Four Seminars on the Astrology of the Red Planet, Centre for Psychological Astrology Press: London, 2001, p. 91.

108   See, "Solar System Exploration: Planets," availabale at
      http://solarsystem.nasa.gov/planets/profile.cfm?Object=J
      upiter&Display=OverviewLong.

109   Id.

110   A.T. Mann, The Round Art of Astrology, cited above, p.
      83; Adam Gainsburg, Sacred Marriage Astrology, cited
      above, p. 298.

111   A.T. Mann, The Round Art of Astrology, p. 83; Adam
      Gainsburg, Sacred Marriage Astrology, p. 316.

112   David McCann, "The Birth of the Outer Planets," avail-
      able at www.skyscript.co.uk/Uranus/html. As stated in
      the article, McCann "is an expert on the history and phi-
      losophy of astrology." The article first appeared in the Tra-
      ditional Astrologer magazine.

113   Uranus can at times be seen without the benefit of a tele-
      scope, but it was not officially recognized as a planet until
      1781. When William Herschel first observed the planet,
      he was convinced that it was a comet. He maintained
      this belief until at least April or November 1781. Ellis
      D. Miner, Uranus: The Planet, Rings and Satellites, Ellis
      Horword: Chichester, UK, 1990, pp. 17 – 21.

114   Ellis D. Miner, Uranus: The Planet, Rings and Satellites,
      p. 22; Heather Couper and Nigel Henbest, The History
      of Astronomy, Firefly Books: China, 2007, p 185; Wil-
      liam Herschel, "Voyager at Uranus," NASA JPL 400-268
      7/85, archived from the original in 2006; Charles Q. Choi,
      "Uranus's History and Naming," Space.com, 9 November
      2010. It is also somewhat unclear that Herschel was en-
      tirely convinced that Georgium Sidus was the best name
      for the planet. He was apparently nudged in this direction

by The Royal Society which was "intent on securing royal assistance for Herschel's research," and "saw a good public relations opportunity slipping away." Mark Littman, Planets Beyond: Discovering the Outer Solar System, John Wiley & Sons: New York, 1990, p. 10.

115 Francisca Herschel, "The Meaning of the Symbol H+O for the Planet Uranus," The Observatory, Vol. 40, pp.306-307, available at http://adsabs.harvard.edu/abs/1917Obs....40..306H. Citing her letter dated 18 July 1917, Ms. Herschel states "the little line above the 'globe' [in the Uranus' glyph] is nothing more than the link that associates Uranus with H, thus combining the name chosen by the German Astronomer, Bode, with that preferred by the French astronomer, De la Lande."

116 Mark Littman, Planets Beyond: Discovering the Outer Solar System, cited above, p. 10.

117 Ellis Miner, Uranus: The Planet, Rings and Satellites, cited above, p. 23. Miner notes that the acceptance of this name was not "universally accepted until after Herschel's death in 1822," p. 23; R. F. Sanford, "The Planet Uranus," Astronomical Society of the Pacific Leaflets, Vol. 4, No. 183, p. 253-255, reprinted at SAO/NASA Astrophysics Data System, available at http://adsabs.harvard.edu/full/1944ASPL....4..254S and http://www.spacestation-info.com/uranus-discovery.htm. It is also interesting to note that William Herschel's death took place on 25 August 1822, just short of his 84th birthday (15 November 1738)– which made his life almost exactly the length of one Uranian orbital revolution. See, Mark Littman, Planets Beyond: Discovering the Outer Solar System, p. 12.

118   James Herschel Holden, A History of Horoscopic Astrology, cited above, pp. 201-202.

119   Kim Farnell, "When and Why did Uranus Become Associated with Aquarius?" January 2005, available at http://www.skyscript.co.uk/ur_aq.html. This article summarizes a Skyscript Forum that took place in December, 2003. She states, "[t]he 1780's were hardly a high point for astrological journalism." p. 1.

120   Id. p. 202, citing Alfred T. Story, Life of John Varley (Richard Bentley: London? [Holden's question mark], 1894.

121   Kim Farnell, "When and Why did Uranus Become Associated with Aquarius?" cited above. With a combination of humor and astrological acumen, Farnell states that it is interesting that Uranus, or *Georgium Sidus*, was "well matched to a king ousted from power on account of his mental instability. . . ."

122   Id. Farnell refers to A.J. Pearce's (*Zadkiel*) Text Book of Astrology published in 1879 and Sepharial's Manual of Astrology (1898) that took issue with the Uranus-Aquarius connection. As late as 1909, Alan Leo (in Everybody's Astrology) acknowledged that Uranus had not yet been given a sign by astrologers, although Aquarius had often been suggested.

123   Except where specifically noted, the factual recitations in this section are taken from several sources: (1) Patrick Moore, The Planet Neptune, Ellis Horwood Ltd.: Chichester, England, 1988; (2) Nicholas Kollerstrom, "The Naming of Neptune," Journal of Astronomical History and Heritage, Vol. 12(1), 66-71 (2009), available at http://www.dioi.org/kn/NeptuneName.pdf; (3) Nicholas

Kollerstrom, "Neptune's Discovery: The British Case for Co-Prediction," October, 2001, available at http://www.dioi.org/kn/neptune/index.htm - this article is divided into several titled sections which I will enumerate where relevant, along with the reference "The British Case;" (4) J. Lequeux, "Chapter 2: The Discovery of Neptune (1845-1846)," in Le Verrier – Magnificent and Detestable Astronomer, Astrophysics and Space Science Library, 397, DOI 10.1007/978-1-4614-555-3_2, Springer Science: New York, 2013; (5) William Sheehan, Nicholas Kollerstrom and Craig B. Waff, "The Case of the Pilfered Planet: Did the British Steal Neptune?," Scientific American, December, 2004; and (6) Mark Littman, Planets Beyond: Discovering the Outer Solar System, cited above, pp. 31 - 60. Throughout the Neptune-related citations, I will not match each factual assertion with a citation unless there is some controversy, it requires emphasis or it represents a particularly germane comment by the author.

124 Nicholas Kollerstrom, "The Naming of Neptune," at p. 69.

125 The articles within Nicholas Kollerstrom's "Neptune's Discovery: The British Case for Co-Prediction " that make this case most strongly include: "The Retrospective Construction of History," "Challis' Unseen Testimony," "Airy Tells the Truth," and "Eggen Takes the Papers."

126 William Sheehan, et al, "The Case of the Pilfered Planet," taken from the title and p. 94.

127 The specific date of the Neptune-Jupiter conjunction was 30 July 1612. Galileo's observations are discussed in an article written by American astronomer, and discoverer of Chiron, Charles Kowal, "Galileo's Observations of Nep-

tune, The International Journal of Scientific History, December, 2008, pp. 3-5, available at http://www.dioi.org/vols/wf0.pdf.

123 Patrick Moore in The Planet Neptune, pp. 15-16 gives one of the clearest explanations of Titius-Bode that I have found. "Take the numbers 0, 3, 6, 12, 24, 48, 96, 192 and 384, each of which (apart from the first two) is double its predecessor. Add 4 to each. Taking the Earth's distance from the Sun as 10, the distances of the planets, out as far as Uranus, are represented with tolerable accuracy." In comparing distance per Titius-Bode and the actual distance, he cites: "Mercury at Titus Bode 4 – actual distance at 3.9, Venus at 7 and 7.2, Earth at 10 and 10.0, Mars at 16 and 15.2, Jupiter at 52 and 52.0, Saturn at 100 and 95.4, Uranus at 196 and 191.8. Ceres' relationship is 28 and 27.7." It was, of course, Neptune which eventually disproved Titius-Bode.

129 J. Lequeux, L Verrier – Magnificent and Detestable Astronomer, p. 49. It is important to note that at least with respect to Le Verrier's "discovery" of Neptune, this title is tongue-in-cheek. Lequeux supports Le Verrier's point of view.

130 Id., p. 26.

131 William Sheehan, et al, "The Case of the Pilfered Planet," p. 97; Mark Littman, Planets Beyond: Discovering the Outer Solar System, cited above, p. 33.

132 Patrick Moore, The Planet Neptune, p. 17.

133 J. Lequeux, L Verrier – Magnificent and Detestable Astronomer, p 47; Mark Littman, Planets Beyond: Discovering the Outer Solar System, cited above, p. 32.

134 William Sheehan, et al, "The Case of the Pilfered Planet,"
     p. 95.

135 Patrick Moore, <u>The Planet Neptune</u>, p. 17. Moore re-
     counts the tale that Airy once spent a day in the Green-
     wich Observatory's cellar labeling empty boxes "empty."
     Also, even when the rain fell and clouds obscured their
     view of the sky, Airy reportedly walked around the Obser-
     vatory, making sure that observers were at their designated
     observing posts. In 1976, Isaac Asimov described Airy as
     "a conceited, envious, small-minded person who ran the
     Greenwich Observatory like a petty tyrant [who] was ob-
     sessed with detail and invariably missed the big picture."
     William Sheehan, et al, "The Case of the Pilfered Planet,"
     p. 93.

136 Interestingly, Airy's wife confirmed that "a" note had been
     left by Adams. See, Nicholas Kollerstrom, "The 'Crown
     Jewels' Document," from "The British Case;" William
     Sheehan, et al, "The Case of the Pilfered Planet," p. 97.
     Mrs. Richarda Airy had a "lot on her mind," as a week
     later she gave birth to their son Osmund. Mark Littman,
     <u>Planets Beyond: Discovering the Outer Solar System</u>,
     cited above, p. 38.

137 The pertinent language from Airy's note is as follows:
     "But I should be very glad to know whether the assumed
     perturbations will explain the error of radius vector of
     Uranus. This error is now very considerable as you will
     be able to ascertain by comparing the normal equations,
     given in the Greenwich Observations each year, for the
     time <u>before</u> opposition with the times <u>after</u> opposition."

(emphasis in text; Nicholas Kollerstrom, "Selected Excerpts of Correspondence, Concerning the Discovery of Neptune," from "The British Case.")

138 Mark Littman, <u>Planets Beyond: Discovering the Outer Solar System</u>, p. 39. Littman contends that from Adams' point of view, he had specified the location of the planet disturbing Uranus' orbit so Uranus' orbit (i.e. Neptune) was "essentially irrelevant"; See, Nicholas Kollerstrom, "Adams Dated Computations" from "The British Case." Kollerstrom is characterizing the general response to Airy's query, but that is not how Kollerstrom views Airy's request of Adams.

139 Nicholas Kollerstrom, "Adams Dated Computations" from "The British Case."

140 Recent scholarship would suggest that Adams began a letter to Airy in November 1845, but apparently did not finish, nor send it. Nicholas Kollerstrom, "Adams Dated Computations" from "The British Case," William Sheehan, et al, "The Case of the Pilfered Planet," p. 98.

141 Patrick Moore, <u>The Planet Neptune</u>, p. 26.

142 J. Lequeux, <u>L Verrier – Magnificent and Detestable Astronomer</u>, p 47; Nicholas Kollerstrom, "Mapless in Cambridge" from "The British Case."

143 Patrick Moore, <u>The Planet Neptune</u>, p. 24.

144 <u>The Cambridge Illustrated History of Astronomy</u>, ed. Michael Hoskin, Cambridge University Press: Cambridge, UK, 2000, p. 193; Nicholas Kollerstrom, "Mapless in Cambridge" from "The British Case." Kollerstrom is dubious about Challis' defense. It is also important to note

that the <u>Illustrated History of Astronomy</u> comes from Cambridge.

145 J. Lequeux, <u>Le Verrier – Magnificent and Detestable Astronomer</u>, p. 25.

146 William Sheehan, et al, The Case of the Pilfered Planet, p. 99; <u>The Cambridge Illustrated History of Astronomy</u>, p. 193; J. Lequeux, <u>Le Verrier – Magnificent and Detestable Astronomer</u>, pp. 43 and 49; Patrick Moore, <u>The Planet Neptune</u>, p. 20. Moore references a comment made by Le Verrier's contemporaries that "although he may not have been the most detestable man in France, [Le Verrier] was certainly the most detested."

147 This was the first of 3 papers given by LeVerrier regarding the entity that was perturbing Uranus' orbit. The first was given to the Paris Academy of Sciences on 10 November 1845, but it essentially set out the problem. The second paper was presented on 1 June 1846, and stated that the irregularities of Uranus' orbit had to be caused by an unknown planet farther from the Sun. The third and final paper was present on 31 August 1846, "laying out the orbital elements, the mass, and the position of the planet that was disturbing Uranus." Mark Littman, <u>Planets Beyond: Discovering the Outer Solar System</u>, pp. 42-46.

148 Patrick Moore, <u>The Planet Neptune</u>, p. 22.

149 Id. p. 23.

150 Nicholas Kollerstrom, "The Naming of Neptune," p. 66, citing Galle.

151 Id. p. 67.

152 Id. p. 67. The vertical line of the "L" matches the left line of the "V" and tilting it slightly to the right, making some-

thing of a Cartesian plane with the right hand "V" placed at a 45° angle. A small trident is placed vertically in the middle of the L-V figure, beginning with a small bulb below the horizontal line of the "L," and rising so the trident points vertically, just above the 45° line of the "V."

153   Patrick Moore, The Planet Neptune, pp. 26-27, quotes Herschel, "The remarkable calculations of M. Le Verrier – which have pointed out, as now appears, nearby the true situation of the new planet, by resolving the inverse problem of the perturbations …. But it was known to me, at that time, (I will take the liberty to cite the Astronomer-Royal as my authority), that a similar investigation had been entered into, and a calculation as to the situation of the new planet very nearly coincident with Mr. Le Verrier's arrived at (in entire ignorance of his conclusions), by a young Cambridge mathematician, Mr. Adams; – who will, I hope, pardon this mention of his name (the matter being one of great historical moment), – and who will, doubtless, in his own good time and manner, place his calculations before the public."

154   Id. p. 27.

155   The exact quote from Nicholas Kollerstrom, The Naming of Neptune," p. 68, is as follows:

M. Challis s'exagere tellement le merite du travail clandestin de M. Adams, qu'il attribute, jusq'a un certain point, au jeune geometre de Cambridge le droit de nommer le nouvel aster. Cette pretention ne sera pas accueillie. La public ne doit rien a qui ne lui a rien appris, a qui ne lui a rendu aucun service. Quoi !

156   Id. p. 68.

157 Id. p. 68.

158 Id. p. 69.

159 Nicholas Kollerstrom citing Airy, "The Naming of Neptune," p. 69.

160 Id. p. 69.

161 Nicholas Kollerstrom citing Airy, "The Naming of Neptune," p. 69.

162 The portion of the story is largely taken from William Sheehan, et al, "The Case of the Pilfered Planet;" and Nicholas Kollerstrom, "Eggen Takes the Papers," in "The British Case."

163 The facts in this paragraph are drawn from Deborah Kent, "The Curious Aftermath of Neptune's Discovery, Physics Today, Vol. 64 (12), December, 2011, pp. 46-51, http://dx.doi.org/10.1063/PT.3.1363.

164 James Herschel Holden, A History of Horoscopic Astrology, cited above, pp. 205-206. More specifically, Holden attributes the "prototype formulation" of Neptune's astrological significance to John Ackroyd in Simmonite's Medical Botany, or Herbal Guide to Health, Unknown Publisher: London, 1848. In this text Ackroyd apparently expresses uncertainty about the sign ruling Neptune, stating "incorrectly" that according to Ptolemy it should rule Aquarius.

165 Id. p. 211.

166 Philip Sedgwick, "Astronomy for Astrologers," NorthStar College of Astrological Studies, 2003, p. 67.

167 See, e.g. "NASA's Voyager 1 Approaches Outer Limit of Solar System," AFP News, 27 June, 2013 http://www.google.com/hostednews/afp/article/ALeqM5iaywefK-

Pfgzm_QjL6j0hlUnqtXg?docId=CNG.857f2aa03e51b1
18898f7a0febe1bc08.1a1.

168   Anyone who has attended a workshop or heard Philip
Sedgwick speak will understand that he would entirely
appreciate the judicious sprinkling of humor into these
subjects.

169   Liz Greene, The Outer Planets and Their Cycles: The Astrology of the Collective, CPA Press: London, 2005, pp.
18-20; Steven Forrest, The Inner Sky: How To Make Wis-
er Choices for a More Fulfilling Life, Seven Paws Press:
Borrego Springs, CA, 1988, pp. 127-130; Philip Graves,
"The Significations of Uranus," available at http://www.
skyscript.co.uk/uranus3.html. Liz Greene is, of course,
an eminent astrologer, Jungian analytic psychologist and
author. Steven Forrest's books on astrology are essential
reading for anyone seeking to learn about astrology.

170   Except where otherwise noted, the information on the
physical features of Uranus and Neptune are primarily
drawn from Philip Sedgwick, "Astronomy for Astrologers," cited above, pp. 67-69, and the NASA websites pro-
filing and detailing their characteristics are found under
"Uranus" and "Neptune" at http://solarsystem.nasa.gov/
planets/profile.cfm?Object=SolarSys.

171   A great graphic of this tilt can be found at http://astrono-
my.nmsu.edu/tharriso/ast105/UranusandNeptune.html.

172   Steven Forrest, The Inner Sky, p. 132; Liz Greene, The
Outer Planets and Their Cycles, p. 21.

173   Philip Graves, "The Significations of Neptune," available
at http://www.skyscript.co.uk/neptune3.html .

174   http://starchild.gsfc.nasa.gov/docs/StarChild/teachers/
      densities.html. Density is the ratio of the mass of an ob-
      ject to the volume of space the objects occupies. The for-
      mula is D=M/V. As stated in this website, density will
      determine if you sink or swim in a given liquid.

175   Calvin J. Hamilton, "The Jovian Planets: Uranus and
      Neptune," at Planetshttp://astronomy.nmsu.edu/tharriso/
      ast105/UranusandNeptune.html. Hamilton has a masters
      degree in electrical engineering and designs high quality
      images of celestial bodies. See, http://www.solarviews.
      com/eng/author.htm.

176   Id.

177   Liz Greene, The Outer Planets and Their Cycles, p. 21.

178   "Exploring the Planets: Neptune Facts," Smithsonian
      Air and Science Museum, available at http://airandspace.
      si.edu/exhibitions/exploring-the-planets/online/neptune/
      nept_facts.html.

179   Adam Gainsburg, Sacred Marriage Astrology, cited above,
      p. 317.

180   See Footnote 217 below that discusses the discoveries of
      Ceres, Pallas, Juno and Vesta during 1801-1807, and the
      15 other celestial bodies identified during 1845-1851. Al-
      though they were observed before the discoveries of Ura-
      nus and Neptune, they were not seen as planetary bodies
      – or at least there was significant confusion about what
      they were. This is undoubtedly a subject for additional dis-
      cussion.

181   Eric Burgess, Uranus and Neptune: The Distant Giants,
      Columbia University Press: New York, 1988, p. 50.

182 I have tried to avoid Wikipedia references, but I can claim no knowledge of chemistry. This quotation regarding uranium's qualities can be found at en.wikipedia.org/wiki/Uranium.

183 Steven Forrest, The Inner Sky, cited above, p. 130

184 Gary Caton, personal correspondence, May 2015. The correlation between Uranus' discovery and the use of the guillotine come from him.

185 Nicholas Campion, A History of Western Astrology: Volume II, cited above, p. 183.

186 Id. pp. 205-206.

187 At the risk of over repetition, I cite this mundane information in order to underscore correlations between the naming of Uranus and Neptune with certain events. My assertion is not simply that these correlations exist, but that they in fact establish planetary identity.

188 The information for Uranus' discovery chart is taken from the Astrodienst website and is: 13 March 1781, 22:39 GMT, Bath, United Kingdom; David McCann, "The Birth of the Outer Planets: Uranus," available at http://www.skyscript.co.uk/uranus.html.

189 Kelly Lee Phipps, "Pioneering a Revolution – Uranus Ingress Into Aries," 2011, available at http://www.divineinspirationastrology.com/articles/Pioneering_a_Revolution.pdf.

190 Gary Caton, personal email correspondence, May, 2015. He states "I have taken the classical tack here because it seems to me that you can't get as objective of a view of something using tools that have come about as a result of that very something. For instance, using Pluto as a ruler

in the very chart that demoted him seems illogical." The classical approach also adopts whole house division.

191 All of Gary Caton's references in this article to stars and their respective meanings arise from the work of Bernadette Brady. I heartily recommend that the reader explore the following: Star and Planet Combinations, The Wessex Astrologer Ltd: Bournemouth, England, 2008; Brady's Book of Fixed Stars, Samuel Weiser, Inc.: York Beach, Maine, 1998; Working with the Whole Sky, Introductory Lecture on Visual Astrology, Astrological Association of GB, York, UK conference, Oct 2005; Astro Logos Fixed Star Lecture Series, available at http://www.bernadette-brady.com. Brady has also co-authored a Visual Astrology software package *Starlight* (Zyntara Publications, 2002).

192 Id.

193 Id.

194 Nicholas Campion, The History of Western Astrology: Vol. II, p. 199.

195 Charles Baudelaire (1821-1867), The Salon of 1846, II. What is Romanticism? (1846).

196 James G. Chastain, Encyclopedia of Revolutions of 1848, first published 1997, revised on 1 November 2005 by Chastain and Holly Johnston, available at http://www.ohio.edu/chastain/introduc.htm.

197 Taking Galle's date, Neptune was first observed on 25 September 1846; the first public demonstration of ether as an anesthetic took place on 16 October 1846 at Massachusetts General Hospital. The sky-lit operating theater on the top floor of Massachusetts General derives

its name from this event. See, http://tps.cr.nps.gov/nhl/detail.cfm?ResourceId=249&ResourceType=Building.

198 ABC News, "History of Surgical Anesthesia, 2014, available at http://www.discoveriesinmedicine.com/Enz-Ho/Ether.html#b.

199 Steven Forrest, The Inner Sky, cited above, p. 134.

200 Nicholas Campion, A History of Western Astrology: Vol. II, cited above, p. 229.

201 Id. p. 229.

202 Gary Caton, personal email correspondence, May 2015.

203 Id. He states, ". . . [W]hen we consider the fact that Neptune's discovery is intimately related to Uranus (it was perturbations in Uranus' orbit which led to the discovery) then we have a clue to help us discriminate between these two charts. In the Uranus discovery chart, Mercury is on the star Alpheratz of the constellation Andromeda and in the Neptune discovery chart, we find Uranus on this same star. Alpheratz is part of a complex mythos that relates to several other nearby constellations –Cassiopeia, Cepheus, Cetus, Perseus and Andromeda. In the Cancer rising chart for the Neptune discovery, we find the stars of Cetus and Pegasus culminating. Because of this connection, I feel the Cancer rising chart says more about the intrinsic nature of Neptune as an archetype.

204 David McCann, "The Birth of The Outer Planets: Neptune," available at http://www.skyscript.co.uk/neptune.html.

205 Gary Caton, personal email correspondence, May 2015.

206 Id.

207 Id.

208 Chris Brennan's lecture is available through www.Chris-BrennanAstrologer.com. It is titled "Uranus, Neptune and the History of Western Astrology," and was given on Saturday, 9 November 2013 in Denver, CO.

209 Gary Caton, personal email correspondence, 4 December 2013.

210 Id.

211 Those familiar with newly discovered objects may notice that I have not discussed the discovery of Ceres, Pallas, Juno and Vesta during 1801-1807, nor the 15 other celestial bodies identified during 1845-1851. I have not done so because of the inherent confusion about what these bodies were at the time of their discovery. This topic warrants further consideration. It is also the case and as is discussed below, that Ceres in particular provides another excellent illustration of both a parochially-laden naming process and a strong correlation with contemporary global developments involving social change.

The Titius-Bode Law (1772) and Uranus' perturbations unleashed a planetary search that not only resulted in the discovery of Neptune, but Ceres as well. The search was in fact so intense that Baron Franz Xavier von Zach, astronomer of the Duke of Gotha and Director of the Seeberg Observatory, had in 1800 formed a group of astronomers, the "Lilienthal Detectives," each of whom were assigned a area of the sky and instructed to look for the missing planet. The Italian astronomer Guiseppe Piazzi made his discovery of Ceres on 1 January 1801, and mailed the news of his discovery to the Italian astronomer Barnaba Oriani and Johan Elert Bode, an astronomer at the Berlin Observatory. It appears that Piazzi advised Oriani that he had discovered a planet, but his letter to Bode was somewhat ambiguous on this point. Piazzi denied this characterization. After doing his own calculations, Bode concluded that the body was in fact the missing planet and announced to the Prussian Academy of Sciences that a new planet "Juno" had been discovered. A naming dispute ensued. Baron von Zach preferred "Hera," but Piazzi had chosen the name "*Ceres Ferdinande,*" although not in honor of the Roman goddess Ceres, but in recognition of her status as the "guardian divinity of his native Sicily." The "*Ferdinande*" portion of the name referred to Sicilian King Ferdinand III. Ultimately, the German astronomers accepted the name of Ceres. [This information is taken from Mark Littman, Planets Beyond: Discovering the Outer Solar System, cited above, pp. 15-22; G. Fodera Serio, A. Manera, and P. Sicoli, " Giuseppe Piazzi and the Discovery of Ceres," Lunar and Planetary Institute: Houston, TX, available at http://www.lpi.usra.edu/books/AsteroidsIII/pdf/3027.pdf.]

In terms of physical features corresponding to her name, Ceres shares the kind of consonances that are associated with the classical and modern planets. [See, http://solar-system.nasa.gov/planets/profile.cfm?Object=Dwa_Ceres.]

She is the largest and most massive asteroid in the belt between Mars and Jupiter, which ties in with Ceres' agricultural and maternal largesse. She displays herself with a motherly, "nearly round body," and "shares characteristics of the rocky, terrestrial planets of our inner solar system."

It is also interesting to note that astronomers describe Ceres as an "embryonic" planet due to the gravitational perturbation of Jupiter that throughout the eons has prevented her from becoming a "full-fledged" planet. [Id.]

In a similar vein as with Uranus and Neptune, global movements of social change are associated with Ceres' discovery. The strongest argument supporting her designation lies in its parallel with the Women's Rights Movement. The changes this movement advanced were profound, and are still being metabolized today. Many of us may think of the 1960s as the start of the Women's Movement, but the world's first women's rights convention was held in Seneca Falls, New York in 19-20 July 1848. In 1792, the British author Mary Wollstonecraft argued for the equality between the sexes in her book, The Vindication of the Rights of Women. Lucretia Mott was born in 1793, Elizabeth Cady Stanton in 1815, and Susan B. Anthony in 1820. [See, Mary M. Huth, "US Suffrage Movement Timeline, 1792 to Present," February, 1995, available at http://www.rochester.edu/sba/suffragetimeline.html. Ms. Huth was a librarian at the Department of Rare Books and Special Collections, University of Rochester Libraries.] These events undeniably support the identity of Ceres, but relate to Pallas, Juno and Vesta as well.

212 Paul Rincon (BBC News science reporter), "The girl who named a planet". _Pluto: The Discovery of Planet X_ (BBC News), retrieved 12 April 2007. The reference to the "agent of annihilation" is taken from Alan Oken, Complete Astrology: The Classic Guide to Modern Astrology, Ibis Press: Berwick, MA, 2006, p. 29. The analogy to

dreams coming true comes, of course, from the "Over the Rainbow" song written for the 1939 movie <u>The Wizard of Oz</u>.

213   David McCann, "The Birth of The Outer Planets: Pluto," available at http://www.skyscript.co.uk/pluto.html.

214   Id.

215   <u>The Cambridge Illustrated History of Astronomy</u>, ed. Michael Hoskin, cited above, p. 284

216   Paul Rincon, "The girl who named a planet," cited above. Venetia Phair (nee Burney) is now a retired teacher from Epsom in Surrey, United Kingdom. Mark Littman, <u>Planets Beyond: Discovering the Outer Solar System</u>, cited above at pp. 84-85.

217   It also appears that contrary to popular myth, astronomer William Herschel may not have coined the term "asteroid." Instead, it was the "son of a poet friend of Herschel's, Greek scholar Charles Burney Jr." who came up with it. As stated by Florida astronomer Clifford Cunningham at the 45th annual convention of the astronomical society's Division of Planetary Sciences in Denver, CO, "Asteroid was Herchel's choice, but it was not his creation." Robert Nolin, Sun Sentinel, 8 October 2013, available at <u>http://articles.sun-sentinel.com/2013-10-08/news/fl-asteroid-word-origin-20131008_1_asteroid-word-planetary-sciences#.Usr2qDjqY3k.email</u>. Other than its intrinsic interest, the reason for the inclusion of this citation here is that one can see the nexus between the astronomical community and the Burney family.

218   Id.

219   Adam Gainsburg, <u>Sacred Marriage Astrology</u>, cited above,
       p. 318.

220   Steven Forrest, <u>The Inner Sky</u>, cited above, p. 137.

221   I must admit that it is difficult not to take note that the
       New Horizons spacecraft approached Pluto as the Plu-
       to-Uranus square had begun to end on 16 March 2015
       (exact). See, Nick Anthony Fiorenza, "Revolution and
       Revelation: Uranus-Pluto Square 2012-2015," available
       at http://www.lunarplanner.com/Uranus-Pluto-Square/
       index.html.

222   The intense competition, machinations and transfor-
       mative renewals that took place with the New Horizon
       Project strongly evoke Pluto's presence, as do a number
       of connections to hidden and fluctuating resources (or
       government funding). A full and fascinating rendition of
       this history is set forth in "First Mission to Pluto: Policy,
       Politics, Science and Technology in the Origins of New
       Horizons, 1989-2003, Historical Studies in the Natural
       Sciences 44 (2014), 234-27, available in an Abstract at
       Michael Neufeld, "First Mission to Pluto: The Difficult
       Birth of New Horizons," Smithsonian Magazine, 10 July
       2015. A brief summary follows.

       In 1989, a "dozen planetary scientists" who called them-
       selves the "Pluto Underground," including Dr. Alan Stern,
       an astrophysicist and principal investigator for what even-
       tually became to be known as the New Horizons mission,
       strategized about how to fly a spacecraft to Pluto. See, Eric
       Betz, "How'd We Get New Horizons? You Can Thank the
       Pluto Underground," Astronomy, 24 June 2015. There was
       urgency in fully committing to the project because Pluto

had already started to move away from the Sun, which would make it more difficult to accomplish the flyby. The 1990's brought a time period where Pluto jockeyed with other "increasingly ambitious" planetary projects for funding. There were also significant debates within the scientific community about whether the project required a "powerful and expensive booster," a smaller spacecraft ("Pluto-350," named for its "approximate dry [unfueled] mass target of 350 kg", Neufeld in "First Mission," at p. 242), or a micro-spacecraft that was essentially a camera set on a space-capable platform ("Pluto Fast Flyby project"). The California Institute of Technology that managed the Jet Propulsion Lab for NASA favored the larger spacecraft; the Applied Physics Lab of Johns Hopkins University, paired with Southwest Research Institute, went for the smaller. Internecine politicking continued throughout the period among NASA administrators and scientists, as well as the larger scientific community. The federal executive and legislative branches of the US government also joined in the fray.

In 1992, the new NASA Administrator and politically well-connected Daniel Goldin arrived in office "convinced that the agency's space-science directorate was ponderous, slow, and wedded to huge and expensive "Battlestar Galactica" spacecraft." (Neufeld in "First Mission," at p. 247). The politics between Pluto-350 and PFF raged, and in 1994 Alan Stern went to Moscow to see if the project would fare better, but given other space project failures, by 1996 Moscow's appetite for the project waned. By 1999 and back in the U.S. the Pluto mission began to gain some steam but at the same time began to compete with a mission to Europa. In September 2000, NASA canceled the Pluto project. In announcing this decision at a press conference, NASA's Associate Administrator Dr. Ed Weiler said, "'We're out of the Pluto business. It's over. It's dead. It's dead. It's dead.'" See, Kenneth Chang, "The Long, Strange Trip to Pluto and How NASA Nearly Missed It," 18 July 2015, available at nytimes.com. This certainly sounds a lot like Pluto!

By this time the window for a Pluto mission had become even more acute because the mission had to launch before December 2005, or the spacecraft would not reach Jupiter in time to use its gravitational pull to boost it to Pluto. Not to be deterred, the planetary science community fomented a "rebellion" (Neufeld Abstract) against NASA's decision to cancel, and in December, 2000, NASA announced that the project was on again. However, when George W. Bush took office as President of the United States in 2002, its administration's budget office quickly canceled Pluto in favor of Europa. At the last moment, U.S. Senator Barbara A. Mikulski of Maryland inserted an earmark in the budget to keep the mission going.

Another Plutonian feature of the New Horizons mission is that its success depended on long periods when the spacecraft "slept," or "went underground." At the appropriate times, it would come back to life. The spacecraft's power largely came from solar panels and batteries, but plutonium – *Pluto-onium* – was also needed to power it when these sources were no longer available. All seemed to be going fairly well, but in August 2004 the Department of Energy informed the New Horizons project that it could not supply the requisite plutonium. Again, a Plutonian dilemma! By reducing the equipment on the spacecraft, it was determined that the Department of Energy could make a lesser but sufficient delivery of plutonium. Thus regenerated, all seemed to be on track with the 19 January 2006 launch, but just after the Jupiter flyby, the New Horizons computer crashed. In fact, the computer crashed about once a year, but managed to restart each time. Again, all seemed to be going well, but on 4 July 2015, which was 10 days after the Jupiter flyby, the spacecraft "suddenly fell silent." (Chang) The computer eventually restarted, but it was unclear whether there was enough time to execute the commands which were needed to guide New Horizons through the flyby. "With hours to spare," the spacecraft was operational and Pluto was revealed in all its glory.

223   See the NASA web site at: http://solarsystem.nasa.gov/planets/profile.cfm?Object=Pluto&Display=OverviewLong.

224   Kenneth Chang, "What We've Learned About Pluto," Science, 17 March 2016, available at nytimes.com.

225   "Frozen Plains in the Heart of Pluto's 'Heart,'" ed. Sarah Loff, 30 July, 2015; "Pluto's Heart: Like a Cosmic 'Lava Lamp,'" ed. Tricia Talbert, 1 June 2016. Available at nasa.gov website.

226   "Pluto's Fretted Terrain," ed. Tricia Talbert, 19 May 2016. Available at nasa.gov website.

227   "Icy 'Spider' on Pluto," ed. Tricia Talbert, 7 April 2016. Available at nasa.gov website.

228   Ray Villard (Space Telescope Science Institute, Balti-
      more, MD) and Marc Buie (Southwest Research Insti-
      tute, Boulder, CO), "New Hubble Maps of Pluto Show
      Surface Changes". HubbleSite News Release Number:
      STScI-2010-06. 4 February 2010. Retrieved 10 February
      2010.

229   The five Moons include: (1) Charon – the mythological
      ferryman who carries the souls of the newly deceased to
      Hades, (2) Nix – a rather mysterious goddess of the night
      (http://www.theoi.com/Protogenos/Nyx.html), (3) Hydra
      - a monster of the swamps (http://theochem.chem.rug.nl/
      resources/Mythica.html), (4) Kerberos or Cerberus– the
      "gigantic hound" who guarded the gates of Hades (http://
      www.theoi.com/Ther/KuonKerberos.html) and (5) Styx –
      the river Charon crosses. The "theoi" web citations refer to
      Theoi Greek Mythology: Exploring Mythology in Clas-
      sical Literature and Art, created and edited by Aaron J.
      Atsma, Auckland, Australia.

230   A barycenter is the center or balance point of the mass of
      two or more bodies, usually celestial bodies.

231   The record this discovery was commemorated by his award
      of the Nobel Prize in Physiology / Medicine in 1945. See,
      http://www.nobelprize.org/nobel_prizes/medicine/laure-
      ates/1945/fleming-bio.html.

232   See The Edwin Powell website at http://edwinhubble.
      com/hubble_bio_001.htm, last modified in 2002.

233   There is some question about who should obtain credit for
      the splitting of the atom, as it appears that several labora-
      tories were working on it at the time. See, a reprint of an
      October 1939 edition of Scientific American regarding a

conference when nuclear fission was announced, available at http://blog.modernmechanix.com/splitting-the-atom/. The Manhattan Project that culminated in the atomic bomb was in operation from 1939-1946.

234   See, http://www.nobelprize.org/nobel_prizes/physics/laureates/1918.

235   The factual assertions and quotations in this paragraph regarding Heisenberg are taken from: David C. Cassidy, "Heisenberg, Uncertainty, and the Quantum Revolution," The Scientific American, May 1992, pp. 106-112. Cassidy is an associate professor of Hofstra University and received the 1992 American Institute of Physics Science Writing Award in Physics and Astronomy for his writing in this area.

236   Robert Hand, "On Creating a Science of Astrology," Essays on Astrology, Whitford Press: Atglen, PA, 1982, pp. 55-61, at p. 61.

237   Sigmund Freud published Interpretation of Dreams in 1900; Carl Jung began his departure from Freud's influence in 1913; John Watson published Psychology, From the Standpoint of a Behaviorist in 1919. Jean Piaget published The Moral Judgment of Children in 1932; in 1942, Carl Rogers published Counseling and Psychotherapy. See, http://psychology.about.com/od/psychology101/a/timeline.htm.

A notable representative of the existentialist movement is Jean-Paul Sartre (1905-1980. His book Being and Nothingness (1943) is representative of this philosophy, and was significantly impacted by his World War II experiences. For a general discussion of existentialism, see

Crowell, Steven, "Existentialism", *The Stanford Encyclopedia of Philosophy* (Winter 2010 Edition), Edward N. Zalta (ed.), available at http://plato.stanford.edu/archives/win2010/entries/existentialism/.

238   Richard Tarnas, Cosmos and the Psyche: Intimations of A New World View, A Plume Book: New York, 2007, p. 50.

239   A good, easy-to-access summary regarding this image and the impact that it had is available at Frances Newman M. Naumann Fine Art: The Armory Show 2013, "Marcel Duchamp", available at www.galleryintell.com.

240   Nicholas Campion, A History of Western Astrology: Vol. II, cited above, pp. 252. Campion's recitation of the circumstances surrounding the publication of Princess Margaret's birth chart is well worth looking into. Id., pp. 259-260. According to Campion, the newspaper had asked "the flamboyant society astrology and hand-reader Cheiro" to read the horoscope. Cheiro claimed as his clients the actress Sarah Bernhardt and King Edward VII, but he was "unavailable" and the feature was actually written by his assistant, R.H. Naylor, "who had built up a reputation lecturing in London theatres." P. 259. Among other items, Naylor stated that "'events of tremendous importance to the Royal Family will come about near her seventh year [1937], and these events will indirectly affect her own fortunes.'" P. 260, citing Naylor's article in the Sunday Express. As noted by Campion, King Edward VII abdicated in that year which was "as shattering an event as the British monarchy had known since the removal of James II in 1689." Also in 1937, Margaret's father was coronated King George VI. This meant that Princess Margaret was

elevated to second in line to the throne. Id., p. 260. Naylor's forecast was "astrologically orthodox" and was based on the movement of the progressed sun to a 90° aspect of Saturn. Id. p. 260.

241   The information regarding Pluto's discovery chart is taken from the Astrodienst website and is: 18 February 1930, GMT 23:00, Flagstaff, Arizona.

242   These 12th house adjectives are taken from Deborah Houlding, The Houses: Temples of the Sky, The Wessex Astrologer: Bournemouth, England, 2006, p. 54.

243   Gary Caton, personal correspondence, May 2015.

244   Id.

245   Gary Caton, cited above.

246   Bernadette Brady, Brady's Book of Fixed Stars, cited above, p. 248.

247   Gary Caton, cited above.

248   Bernadette Brady, Brady's Book of Fixed Stars, cited above, p. 198.

249   In choosing to identify Copernicus with this paradigm shift, I am mindful that there are a number of candidates at least as worthy as Copernicus. At one level my choice is one of convenience, as well as the fact that most people assume that it was the "Copernican Revolution" which fundamentally "deposed man from his privileged position at the heart of the cosmos." Nicholas Campion, History of Western Astrology: Volume II: The Medieval and Modern Worlds, cited above, p. 111. Campion takes issue with this "frequently repeated cliché[s]" and asserts that instead of "liberating" humanity, Copernicus' placement of the Sun in fact consolidated extant religious and cultural beliefs

regarding the spiritual centrality of the Sun. According to Campion, Copernicus "came not to bury the old cosmos but to save it." Id, p. 111. As might be expected, Campion's arguments are persuasive, but he also states that instead of tinkering around the edges with different measuring methods or tools, Copernicus' "genius" was to see that the problem with planets that were not moving in accordance with Platonic, circular perfection lay not in the nature of measurement but that the underlying model was wrong. Id, p. 109. (Emphasis added.) I would argue that regardless of Copernicus' intent, by re-drawing celestial drawing boards, both Copernicus' solution and Pluto's demotion triggered fundamental changes. Like the seeding of the New Moon, neither Copernicus nor Pluto may have intended it, but that is what happened.

There are a number of other candidates whose insights were ground-breaking. As stated by Campion, Isaac Newton's (1642-1727) conclusions rose to the level of a "seismic intellectual earthquake," whereby "modernity received its ideological underpinning in a universe which was to be entirely explicable by mechanical forces, with no need for deity, divinity, demons or angels." Id, p. 177. Johannes Kepler's (1571-1630) discovery that planetary orbits traced an elliptical, as opposed to perfectly circular paths also represents a major step forward in apprehending the solar system. Campion legitimately characterizes Galileo Galilei's (1564-1642) ideas as "laying the foundation of modern physics." Id, p. 146. While not gainsaying the profound significance of these ideas, it was still Copernicus (1473-1543) who, however unwittingly, rocked the boat.

Both Pluto and Copernicus shifted foundations in a way that got people thinking in a paradigmatically novel way.

250 James Hillman, The Dream and the Underworld, Harper Perennial: New York, NY, 1979, at p. 53.

251 Needless to say, I am not advocating entering into the "influence" versus "association" or "correlation" debate here. Most people today believe that astrology is talking about the former, and it is to that belief that I generally direct my comments in this section. I would guess that most of today's astrologers lie in the second camp. In the spirit of full disclosure, I am not sure where I land in the debate. No, I do not believe Jupiter places kings on thrones or Venus dictates with whom we should fall in love. On the other hand, "influence" and "association" suggest list making, which removes the ineffability of the celestial connection with human beings. And I use the term "being" advisedly, in all the profound levels that the word connotes.

252 The balance of this paragraph reproduces Stern's fascinating UTube video which is available at http://www.youtube.com/watch?v=8Nk2LF22W64.

253 This paradigm shift is also recognized by Michael E. Brown, How I Killed Pluto and Why It Had It Coming, cited above, pp. 27-28.

254 Id.

255 NASA characterizes this theory of the Moon's creation as "leading." See, "Earth's Moon: Read More," http://solarsystem.nasa.gov/planets/profile.cfm?Object=Moon&Display=OverviewLong. Other theories hypothesize Earth's gravitational capture and an ancient breakup of the Earth.

See, "Theories of Formation for the Moon," http://csep10.
phys.utk.edu/astr161/lect/moon/moon_formation.html.
An easy-to-read discussion of this debate can also be
found at the NOVA website, http://www.pbs.org/wgbh/
nova/tothemoon/origins.html.

256 Michael E. Brown, "Dwarf Planets are Crazy," available
     at http://www.mikebrownsplanets.com/2010/11/dwarf-
     planets-are-crazy.html; Michael E. Brown, How I Killed
     Pluto and Why It Had It Coming, cited above.

257 Jane Platt, Dolores Beasley, and Robert Tindol, "NASA-
     Funded Scientists Discover Tenth Planet," revised 3 Au-
     gust 2015, available at nasa.gov.; "Eris: Overview," avail-
     able at solarsystem.nasa.gov.

258 Robert Hand, "Uranus-Pluto: A Cycle of Change and
     Revolution," a talk given at the Northwest Astrological
     Conference, 24 May 2014, Seattle, WA. I note that Hand's
     question was raised almost eight years since Pluto's demo-
     tion.

259 I am entirely in agreement with this assertion, but the
     fact that Pluto continues to manifest its power leads me
     to question the nature and implication of its "demotion,"
     rather than sidestep it.

260 William Shakespeare, The Tragedy of Julius Caesar, Act
     III, Scene II – "The Forum," spoken by Antony after his "I
     come to bury Caesar, not to praise him" speech.

261 The press release regarding the IAU vote, which also ref-
     erences its date and time, is available at http://www.iau.
     org/public_press/news/detail/iau0603/.

262 The Pluto reclassification chart here is drawn by using
     whole sign houses.

263   It is also interesting to note that a number of planetary bodies align with the 2nd - 8th house, or 1st and 3rd quadrant, functional oppositions. Vesta and Juno lie conjunct the Moon, Ceres conjoins Neptune, and Mars is conjunct Lilith. Chiron lies in the 1st house, Aquarius. My reference to these planetary bodies is not meant to express an opinion about their astrological significance, but am offering the information in the spirit of open discussion.

264   The conjunction interval between the Sun and Mercury is 7°37"14'.

265   Deborah Houding, The Houses: Temples of the Sky, The Wessex Astrologer Ltd; Bournemouth, England, 1006, pp. 48-49.

266   This correlation between Mercury (also known as Hermes) and astrology was suggested by Gary Caton, personal correspondence, May 2015. I thank him for it, as well as his other insights.

267   We may also note that Chiron rounds out all other planet-like occupants in the 1st quadrant (1st House). I mention it here as many of us place Chiron in our charts as another "outer" planet, although Chiron's actual status as a centaur, and either a minor planet or comet, is discussed below.

268   Gary Caton, personal correspondence, May 2015.

269   I am fully aware that citing Eris as an astrological significator may seem to be antithetical to my thesis. I cite it here due to the fact that some may see Eris as the agent of the restructuring of the solar system and its *sequelae*, rather than Post-Pluto.

270 Ceres also belongs in this list. See analysis of Ceres' discovery above, at endnote 217.

271 This is the conclusion of astronomers Michael E. Brown and Alex Filippenko, cited above in the text and footnotes 9, 11-17. NASA is well aware of this definitional limitation and describes it as the "planethood debate." See, http://solarsystem.nasa.gov/planets/profile.cfm?Object= SolarSys&Display=OverviewLong.

272 See, e.g. "Planet Sizes – Comparison Images and Video," at http://www.funmint.com/planet-sizes-comparison-images-and-video/.

273 This time period also includes the discoveries of Ceres, Pallas, Juno and Vesta (1801-1807). These celestial entities were eventually classified as minor planets, but as will be discussed more fully below, their discoveries and classifications did not herald a fundamental change to the extant celestial paradigm. Pluto's reclassification did.

274 Nicholas Campion, A History of Western Astrology: Volume II, cited above, p. 176. Campion's description of the impact of Isaac Newton's discoveries is well worth reading. He argues that a host of Eighteenth Century cultural and philosophical factors contributed to what can be described as "Newtonianism" or the "doctrine of [a] lifeless, purposeless, mechanical cosmos." Campion acknowledges that Newton's astronomical and mathematical discoveries unquestionably disposed of the idea that planets and zodiac signs "might have personalities," but he adds that Newton was not an "anti-religious materialist." The Newtonian mathematics that established gravity and inertia also defined a universe "filled with divine purpose." Campion

continues by pointing out that Newton "had no interest whatsoever in judicial astrology," and yet he believed "that comets were messages from God, that history unfolded in line with the movement of the constellations. . . . ." Id. p. 177. He also practiced alchemy. Newton's "proof that the universe operates according to a single set of laws implied that people and planets were part of a single system." Id. 177. This conclusion "led to the creation of new forms of astrology, some of which acknowledged that name, while others rejected it." Id, p. 177.

275   Garry Phillipson, "An Interview with Robert Hand," cited above. As articulated by Robert Hand,

". . . [M]ost scientists and other people today assume that reality lies in the object – i.e. that which exists independently of any observer and which can be viewed more or less the same way by any observer. The objectivist considers experiences that are created or conditioned by the nature of the individual to be unreal, imaginary, or at best 'subjective,' i.e. of an inferior order of reality.

Such a view has given rise to a theory of creation in which living organisms are formed solely through the chance interaction of matter and energy. Eventually consciousness comes into being through the same laws of physics, chemistry, and probability that gave rise to organisms. Thus in the modern creation story the object precedes consciousness, and matter and energy precede all."

Another source which thoroughly explores potential connections between contemporary chaos theory and astrology is articulated by Bernadette Brady In Astrology, A Place in Chaos, The Wessex Astrologer: Bournemouth

England, 2006. She points to fractals which "display an inherent quality . . . as a fractal unfolds at any given point, it is unpredictable yet when viewed as a whole, it displays a pattern or shape." (p. 114) She concludes that a "chaotic astrologer" (p. 159) has "an inherent understanding of the total unity of all living and non-living systems." (p. 161). As we can see, chaos theory and fractals are far from mechanistically derived.

276   Robert, Hand "Why Is It So Difficult to Prove Astrology?" This is a lecture given by Hand at a Northern Oregon and Washington Astrology conference.

277   Garry Phillipson, "An Interview with Robert Hand," cited above.

278   Richard Tarnas, PhD, <u>Cosmos and Psyche: Intimations of a New World View</u>, A Plume Book: New York, 2007, p. 73.

279   Nicholas Campion, <u>A History of Western Astrology: Vol. I</u>, pp. 150-151.

280   This dualism lives on today in the contemporary understanding of "transcendence" and "transpersonal." Regrettably, these words are used so casually and in so many settings that they have lost much of their meaning. Particularly for the Western mindset, it is difficult to disengage them from our cultural emphasis on ego and black-and-white (unenlightened versus enlightened) categorizations.

281   Bernadette Brady, <u>Star and Planet Combinations</u>, cited above, p. 1.

282   Id.

283   <u>Charles T. Kowal, Asteroids: Their Nature and Utilization</u>, Ellis Horwood Ltd; Chichester, England, 1988, p. 66

284 Id. P. 66.

285 Id. pp. 17, 66.

286 Elizabeth Powell, "Top 9 Weird Asteroid Names (and 1 Awesome Asteroid Moon Name)," Universe Today, 11 March 2013, available at http://www.universetoday. com/100449/top-9-weird-asteroid-names-and-1-awe- some-asteroid-moon-name/. Howell is the senior writer at Universe Today and works with NASA.

287 Gary W. Kronk, "95P/Chiron," Gary W. Kronk's Come- tography, http://cometography.com/pcomets/095p.html. Kronk is an amateur astronomer and writer. This web site shows pictures of the astronomical sightings of Chiron.

288 International Astronomical Union, "Naming Astro- nomical Objects," available at http://www.iau.org/public/ themes/naming/#minorplanets. NASA defines a comet as "a ball of frozen gases, rock and dust that is about the size of a small town. Comets orbit the sun. Jets of gas and dust from comets form long tails that can be seen from Earth." See, http://www.nasa.gov/audience/forstudents/k- 4/dic- tionary/Comet.html#.VDwnf75Ns9Y . An asteroid is "a rocky object in space that can be a few feet wide to several hundred miles wide. Most asteroids in the solar system orbit in a belt between Mars and Jupiter." See, http:// www.nasa.gov/audience/forstudents/k-4/dictionary/As- teroid.html .

289 NASA Jet Propulsion Lab, "Centaurs in the Solar System," available at http://www.astrobio.net/pressrelease/5585/ centaurs-in-the-solar-system.
See also, Whitney Clavin, "Astronomers Reveal the True Identity of Mysterious Centaurs," SciTechDaily, 26 July

2013, available at http://scitechdaily.com/astronomers-reveal-the-true-identity-of-mysterious-centaurs/. Clavin works at the NASA Jet Propulsion Laboratory.

290 "Chiron, Pholus & Co.," available at http://www.astro.com/astrology/in_chiron_n.htm.

291 Martin Lass, "Chiron's Birth – Chart Delineation," www.dancingwiththestarsastrology.com/chironbirth.htm; 2004. Lass notes that the date chosen for the chart (1 November 1977) might not be correct. My research indicates Chiron's discovery was in October, 1977. His conclusions are nonetheless valid.

292 Barbara Hand Clow, Chiron: Rainbow Bridge Between the Inner and Outer Planets, 2nd ed., Llewellyn Publications: St. Paul, MN, 2008, pp. xiii-xvi.

293 Id.

294 "Response to: Nature of Chiron," ISAR Vol. 800, 27 July 2014

295 Except where particularly germane, the factual assertions regarding Haumea's discovery and naming are taken from: (1) Michael E. Brown, "Haumea," posted 17 September 2008, available at: file:///Users/garnertg/Desktop/CHANGE%20PAPER%20REFS/Haumea/Mike%20Brown's%20Planets:%20Haumea.webarchive, (2) Michael E. Brown, How I Killed Pluto and Why It Had It Coming, cited above; (3) Kelly Beatty, "Haumea: Dwarf-Planet Name Game," Sky and Telescope, February, 2013, available at, http://www.skyandtelescope.com/news/28646964.html; and (4) Cal Fussman, "The Man Who Finds Planets," Discover, May, 2006, available at,

http://discovermagazine.com/2006/may/cover#.Un-FACpFDI9Y.

296   As an aside, it must be recognized that Brown's consid-
       erations about reading his information before making it
       available for public scrutiny are quite salient and real. In
       genuine acknowledgment of the hard work done by the
       astronomical community regarding discoveries of celestial
       bodies, one can only imagine the amount of observational
       and mathematical work that must be performed in order
       to verify the presence and characteristics of distant ob-
       jects. See, e.g. Michael E. Brown, How I Killed Pluto and
       Why It Had It Coming, cited above.

297   See, "IAU Names Fifth Dwarf Planet Haumea,"17 Sep-
       tember 2008, Paris, available at: http://www.iau.org/pub-
       lic_press/news/detail/iau0807/.

298   From 2010 through early 2011, NASA's Wide-Field
       Infrared Survey Explorer ("WISE") performed two full
       scans of the sky. The survey captured images of nearly 750
       million asteroids, stars and galaxies. See, http://www.nasa.
       gov/press/2014/march/nasas-wise-survey-finds-thou-
       sands-of-new-stars-but-no-planet-x/#.U_FdF0tgw9Y .

299   Philip Sedgwick, Astronomy for Astrologers, cited above,
       p. 69.

300   Laeticia Grevers, "The Incan Milky Way: A Path to An-
       other World," cited above.
       Anthony Aveni, Stairways to the Stars, cited above, p 49.

301   Transference relates to a client transferring his or her
       feelings onto someone else, such as the client who thinks
       the astrologer is similar to a parent. Countertransference
       deals with feelings going in the other direction – from

the astrologer or therapist to the client. For example, an astrologer who has a strong Saturn in her or his chart may either skip over or unduly emphasize issues surrounding a client's ability to see things as they are or to take responsibility for actions. The examples are infinite, of course. See, C. G. Jung, Memories, Dreams, Reflections, Alfred A. Knopf and Random House: New York, 1963, in the chapter on "Psychiatric Activities," at pp. 132-133; Ralph R. Greenson, The Technique and Practice of Psychoanalysis, Volume I, International Universities Press, Inc.: New York, 1967.

302 When I speak of science, I do not limit science to test tubes and cyclotrons. I refer instead to making a hypothesis, testing it and re-testing it to ensure validity. The substance of the hypothesis, be it astrological, mechanical, mathematical or wacko, is of no matter. If it works and continues to work, it works. Perhaps a more sophisticated approach, and one more appropriate for our discussion here, is that presented by the behavioral psychologist Stephen Hayes, PhD, et al. He defines science as follows: "From a functional and contextual perspective [Hayes' perspective], scientific analysis is a social enterprise that seeks the development of increasingly organized statements of relations among events that allow analytic goals to be accomplished with *precision, scope, and depth, based on verifiable experience.* . . . [P]recision means that only a limited number of analytic concepts apply to a given case; scope means a given analytic concept applies to a range of cases; and depth means analytic concepts cohere across well-established scientific domains. A bread recipe has

precision but no scope; animism has the opposite problem." Stephen C. Hayes, Dermot Barnes-Holmes, Kelly G. Wilson, "Contextual Behavioral Science: Creating a Science More Adequate to the Challenge of the Human Condition," Journal of Contextual Behavioral Science, Vol. 1, 2012, pp. 1-16, at p. 1, emphasis supplied).

It is important to note that the word "scientific" before "domains" arises because he is specifically talking about "creating a science." Regardless, his point is intriguing and can be applied in a number of realms. Hayes goes on to disavow an effort to attain "truth" in his scientific endeavors, but at the same time emphasizes the importance of developing a "truth criterion" shared by a "social enterprise." For our purposes, it may be that "it works" seems sufficient proof of the validity of astrology because astrologers share a given "truth criterion." But what is that "truth criterion?" That question may encapsulate this entire work and I invite further response to it.

303   Edith Hathaway, "Fixed Stars - Interview with Diana K. Rosenberg," ISAR International Astrologer, pp. 14-25, Leo-2010 issue (print edition); released 22 July 2010 in the on-line version. This article was requested by M. Kelley Hunter for her ongoing column: *Mercury in Sagittarius*. Edith Hathaway was Guest Interviewer for this issue. Also available at http://edithhathaway.com/pdf/DianaKRosenbergInterview.pdf.

304   Id., p. 10.

305   Bernadette Brady, Star and Planet Combinations, The Wessex Astrologer Ltd: Bournemouth, England, 2008; Brady's Book of Fixed Stars, cited above; Working with

the Whole Sky, Introductory Lecture on Visual Astrology, Astrological Association of GB, York, UK conference, Oct 2005; Astro Logos Fixed Star Lecture Series, available at http://www.bernadettebrady.com. Brady has also co-authored a Visual Astrology software package *Starlight* (Zyntara Publications, 2002).

306 Bernadette Brady, <u>Star and Planet Combinations</u>, p. 1.

307 Soulsign Publishing: Burke, Virginia, 2012, cited above.

308 Id., p. 5.

309 This section is taken from Adam Gainsburg, <u>Sky Phases: The Original Planetary Cycles</u>, soulsign.com.

310 Bernadette Brady, <u>Star and Planet Combinations</u>, cited above, p. 1.

311 I note that astrology is not the only subject of scientific derision. In his article "Why Not Just Weigh the Fish?" Robert Pasnau, a professor of philosophy at the University of Colorado, Boulder and the Isaiah Berlin visiting professor in the history of ideas at Oxford University, makes the case that philosophy has also been the "subject of ridicule." I quote: "Morale these days has fallen pretty low along the corridors of philosophy departments. From one side, we get the mockery of the scientists. Freeman Dyson calls philosophy today 'a toothless relic of past glories.' According to Neil deGrasse Tyson, majoring in philosophy 'can really mess you up.' Stephen Hawking declares that 'philosophy is dead.' From another side, we have to cope with the apostasy of our own leading figures. John Searle describes the field as being in 'terrible shape.' Peter Unger says that philosophers are 'under the impression that

they're saying something new and interesting about how it is about the world, when in fact this is all an illusion.'"

Similar comments were seen over 2,000 years ago when Pietro Pomponazzi, a Renaissance philosopher, cautioned his students about choosing philosophy for a career as (1) it did not pay, (2) it "constantly failed to achieve results," and (3) was "more like 'playing with toys." He asks why don't we "stop wasting your time and just weigh that fish?" In order to learn what Pasnau concludes, see his article available at the Opinion pages of the New York Times, 29 June, 2014 edition. or, http://opinionator.blogs.nytimes.com/2014/06/29/why-not-just-weigh-the-fish.

312   Categories included Essentials of Astrology; Forecasting Trends/Cycles; The Astrology of Pragmatic Mysticism, Divination and Applied Myth; Consulting and Healing; East Meets West; Esoteric / Philosophical /Spiritual; Finance and Business; History – Through Time and Culture; Myths and Archetypes; Political and Mundane; Predictive Techniques; Scholarly Papers; Specialties; Symmetrical; Vedic. I would also point to Under the Sky, Rafael Nasser, ed. Jodie Forrest, cited above. Astrologers representing twelve traditions read the same chart. The traditions and respective authors noted in *Under the Sky* include: Asteroid Centered – Demetra George, Archetypal – Evelyn Roberts, Uranian – Gary Christen, Psychological – Hadley Fitzgerald, Modern Wesern – John Marchesella, Ken Bowser – Western Sidereal, Light Hearted – Kim Rogers-Gallagher, Medieval – Robert Hand, Hellenistic – Robert Schmidt, Vedic – Ronnie Dale Dreyer, Evolutionary – Steven Forrest, and Mythological – Wendy Z. Ashley.

313   Stephen C. Hayes, PhD, Dermot Barnes-Holmes PhD and Kelly G. Wilson, PhD, "Contextual Behavioral Science: Creating a Science More Adequate to the Challenge of the Human Condition, cited above, p. 1.

314   Cary Fukunaga, writer, and Nic Pizzolatto, director, True Detective, "Form and Void," Home Box Office, Episode 8, 2014, the concluding dialogue.

ABOUT THE AUTHOR

Patricia Garner received her J.D. from Loyola University School of Law, and her M.S.W. from Portland State University. She describes herself as a "consummate cynic and someone steeped in deductive reasoning," which is reflected in her early career as federal prosecutor and criminal defense attorney. She also taught trial practice at the University of North Carolina School of Law.

She has always been drawn to learning about diverse topics, but never anticipated that astrology would be one. Some thirty years ago, she experienced the profound "whammy" of an astrological chart reading and has never quite looked at the world with the same eyes. Her formal study of astrology took place through the London Faculty of Astrological Studies, but since then she has embarked on an extensive study of the contrasts and commonalities among the truths revealed between a two-dimensional astrological chart and the profound drama embodied in our real sky.